To Naomi xxe

[illegible]

Courtrooms of the Mind

BOOKS I & II

Courtrooms of the Mind

BOOKS I & II

Stories and Advice on Judging Others Favorably

Including halachic references and commentary

by

HANOCH TELLER

New York City Publishing Company

ISBN 0—9614772-4-5

Registered in Library of Congress

12 11 10 9 8 7 6 5 4

Available through:

NYC Publishing Co.
37 W. 37th St. 4th floor
NY, NY 10018

1429 Coney Island Avenue
Brooklyn, N.Y 11230

J. Lehmann
Hebrew Booksellers
20 Cambridge Terrace
Gateshead
Tyne & Wear

Kollel Bookshop
22 Muller St.
Yeoville Johannesburg 2198

To the memory
of the oppressed and downtrodden
whose cases were never even heard
in the courtrooms of our mind.

לעי״נ נפש נקי וצדיק
רבי ישראל לוין ז״ל
שכל ימיו היו
שרשרת של מסירות נפש
לקיום תורה ומצות בטהרה
בימי מגוריו בעמק הבכא
מאחורי מסך הברזל
ובשבתו בארץ הקדש

ת.נ.צ.ב.ה.

ALSO BY HANOCH TELLER

Once Upon a Soul
Soul Survivors
'Souled!'
The Steipler Gaon
Sunset

APPROBATION FROM HAGAON HARAV NOSSON WACHTFOGEL SHLITA

בס״ד

Beth Medrash Govoha

בית · מדרש · גבוה

Rabbi Aaron Kotler Institute for Advanced Learning
617 Sixth Street, Lakewood, NJ 08701 • (201) 367-1060

בשורה רבה היתה זו לי, בהיוודעי כי ש"ב הרב חנוך יונתן טלר שליט"א - סופר יר"ש, פורה ומפרה - מוסיף נדבך לספריתו - ספריתנו. וחזקה על חבר שאינו מוציא מת"י דבר שאינו מתיקן.

משנה יתירא היא להציג את הרב המחבר שליט"א. סדרות ספריו המעולים, כבר הוציאו לו מוניטין באשר, כמעט ואין בית -- מבין דוברי אנגלית -- אשר לא נפוצו שמה. מסויימים הם ספריו בתוכנם, ומופלאים בסגנונם. אף ידועה היא השפעתם הברוכה, בעוררם לב בנים אל אביהם.

מאז, שמחתי בספריו המרעננים. שמחה כפולה באתני בעקב ספרו הנוכחי. הפעם, חידוש מרנין: ספר מוסרי-השקפתי, בשדה לא עובד, "הוי דן את כל האדם לכף זכות." ילקוט ספורי -- על פי מקורות אמינים -- רב לקח, המוגש ביד אמן, בסגנון מעודן ומהנה, הפותח פתח כפתחו של אולם בנושא זנוח זה.

הרינו לברך בזה את ידידי ש"ב הרב המחבר שליט"א בברכת התורה, התחזק וחזק, ויפוצו מעיונתיך חוצה.

בצפיה למשיח צדקנו, ר"ח אלול תשמ"ז

נתן וואכטפוגל

APPROBATION FROM HAGAON HARAV SIMCHA SCHUSTAL SHLITA

ב״ה

Bais Binyomin
Talmudic Research Center
DEDICATED TO THE MEMORY OF BENJAMIN PRUZANSKY ז״ל

ישיבת בית בנימין
ע״ש ר׳ בנימין יהודה הלוי פרוזנסקי ז״ל

Rabbi Simcha Schustal
Rabbi Meyer Hershkowitz
Roshei Hayeshiva

Rabbi Dovid Hersh Mayer
Rabbi Tzvi Pruzansky
Menahalei Hayeshiva

בס״ד

מכתב ברכה

שמחתי מאד לשמוע שמע״כ ידידי הנעלה הרב חנוך יונתן טלר שליט״א,
רחש לבו דבר גדול מאד, ומתכונן בע״ה להוציא לאור עולם בשפה האנגלית
חיבור של סיפורים נפלאים, דוגמאות לקוחות מן החיים, וכתובים
בסגנונו המיוחד והמופלא, לעורר ולהלהיב את הלבבות, למדה הקדושה
והרוממה, שחייבנו בה, לדון את כל אדם לכף זכות, שהוא מפתח
גדול ושמירה גדולה, לקיום כמה וכמה מצות שבין אדם לחבירו בכלל,
ובפרט מניעת קטטות ומריבות, ומשנאת חנם, שבעוונה חרב בעוה״ר
בית מקדשנו, כמאמרם ז״ל במס׳ יומא.

והנה כבר זכה הרב המחבר הנ״ל, לזכות את הרבים
בחיבוריו הקודמים הכתובים באופן הנ״ל, לעורר את הלבבות, לאמונה,
לבטחון, לאהבת ה׳ ותורתו, ולשאר המדות, וברור שבעזהשי״ת יהי׳
גם חיבורו הנ״ל, תועלת גדולה, ולחיזוק [illegible] בהשקפה ולמעשה במדה
הקדושה הנ״ל.

והנה נפשי יודעת מאד, שלא לי להיות מן המסכימים, ובפרט
שכבר הסכימו על חיבוריו, גדולי ומאורי ישראל, הגה״צ שליט״א, אמנם לא
יכולתי לסרב להרה״ג שליט״א, מלבא עכ״פ, בדברי ברכה והוראה, מקרב
ולב עמוק.

ויברכהו השי״ת, שחפץ ה׳ בידו יצליח מאוד, בחיבוריו הנ״ל,
ויזכה להמשיך עוד ועוד בהוצאת ספרי קודש, להרחיב גבול
הקדושה, מתוך מנוחת הנפש, הרחבת הדעת, ברה״ג, וכט״ס בגו״ר,
כחפץ נפשו, ונפש ידידו, הכו״ח ביום [illegible] לחדש מרחשון תשמ״ט, סטאמפארד יצ״ו
אלי׳ שמחה שוסטאל

ONE HUNDRED THIRTY TWO PROSPECT STREET / STAMFORD, CONNECTICUT 06901 / (203) 325-4351

Contents

BOOK I

ב"ה

Introduction

SCENE: A court of law, Mendel on the witness stand, his business partner, Velvel, in the defendant's seat. "He's a crook," Mendel declares. "He was born a crook, he's always been a crook, and he'll die a crook!"

"Objection!" Velvel's lawyer cries.

The judge turns to the court stenographer and asks her to read the testimony. " 'He's a crook,' " she quotes. " 'He was born a crook, he's always been a crook, and he'll die a crook.' " The judge orders her to strike the testimony from the record and instructs the jury to disregard Mendel's outburst.

But it's too late! The damage is done. Velvel's fate will be decided by the jury members not in the court of law but in the courtrooms of their minds. The negative impression was not only made, but reinforced; the words have been struck from the record, but the image has not been erased from their minds. Only by a conscious act of will can the jurors possibly "disregard" the testimony, an act of will that opposes their natural tendency to recall it vividly.

There is no excess verbiage in the Torah. Each word has

a purpose. When we read as small children "Honor your father and mother" we may wonder why it is necessary for the Torah to command us to do that which comes naturally. It is only later on, when our parents' demands conflict with our desires that we begin to comprehend that a conscious act of will is required on our part to overcome our natural tendencies. Similarly, the commandment to "judge favorably" requires such an act of will. And the rewards for obeying this commandment are likewise great.

The stories in *Courtrooms of the Mind*, all of which are true, demonstrate that one who judges others favorably is ultimately vindicated, and that details one might dismiss as inconsequential or absurd aren't inconsequential at all. As these stories illustrate, if one judges favorably, chances are one has judged correctly. And conversely, one who jumps to conclusions, runs the risk of falsely condemning his fellow man. Conscience and reason are the only witnesses for the defense in the courtrooms of the mind.

Imagine elderly Mrs. Goldberg returning from the supermarket, her arms laden with heavy shopping bags. A neighbor waves a friendly hello as he drives right past her in an empty car. Before you condemn the person behind the wheel one additional detail should be mentioned: the driver is *you*.

Only *you* know that just around the corner you will pick up a family of five headed for the airport. Or that you are actually waving at someone else and didn't even notice Mrs. Goldberg. Let's hope Mrs. Goldberg didn't jump to any hasty conclusions about *you!*

This idea was driven home to me most pointedly when my young son returned from *cheder* and announced, "Shmulie pushed me so hard today!"

"What did you do to him? " I asked.

"Nothing."

"Do you mean that Shmulie pushed you for no reason? Did your Rebbe see him do it?"

"Uh huh. Shmulie pushed me right in front of him."

"And he didn't say anything to Shmulie?"

"No. All the other children watched, too."

My paternal instincts shifted into overdrive as I grabbed the phone to call my son's Rebbe to investigate. My boy was so animated about the incident that I was certain that he couldn't have made it up.

As I punched in the number and waited for an answer, he related the story again, this time with slightly more detail: "You should have seen how Shmulie pushed me *in the red wagon,* I rolled all the way across the room!" I confess — I committed the crime of misjudgement and was almost made to suffer the embarrassing consequences. In fact, my crime might have led to false accusations, with consequences worse than my embarrassment — and deservedly so.

Just as I was writing these words, a friend called me on my "story hotline" with an incident in which misjudgment for once had a wonderful outcome.

Mrs. Epstein was waiting in line at the butcher shop and when at last her turn came, two youngsters entered the store. "You won't mind waiting a few more minutes, will you, Mrs. Epstein?" the butcher asked. "I'll be finished with these kids in a moment."

Mrs. Epstein did mind, as she was very tired, but protesting required more of an effort than waiting. She watched as the butcher proceeded to gather chicken legs, gizzards, necks, entrails and other assorted detritus, weigh the entire mess, and scoop it all into a bag. He handed the bag to the children and the older of the two said, "Please put it on our account."

Mrs. Epstein was appalled. Didn't the butcher earn enough without having to charge obviously needy people for the garbage he would have discarded? she thought, indignant. Even if they were only intending to feed the *shirayim* to the dog, he still had no right to take money for trash!

Too weary to engage in a heated discussion, she allowed the issue to pass... until the following week, when precisely the same incident transpired. "How can you do such a thing?" Mrs. Epstein demanded of the butcher.

"I'll tell you, Mrs. Epstein," the butcher replied, leaning on his chopping block, "their mother had been a good customer of mine for many years when suddenly her husband fell ill. He was out of work for a long time and couldn't pay his bills, mine included, but I couldn't allow a family with nine children to starve, could I?

"I carried them for month after month until their account stretched back over three years. It was a tidy sum, believe me! The father, *Rachmana litzlan*, did not get well and frankly I couldn't afford to carry them much longer. There was clearly no point in sending them the bill. So I started to save all the trimmings that would normally be discarded — sometimes I even have a nice piece of lamb that inadvertently got sliced off together with the fat — and give it to them for Shabbos. At least I know they're getting a little decent nourishment.

"And each week, they tell me to put it on their account. And each week I... don't. Oh, sure, I weigh it and make a show of entering the amount in my book, but only to maintain their dignity."

Tears welled up in Mrs. Epstein's eyes — tears of pity for the needy family and tears of shame for misjudging the kindly butcher. She opened her purse and pulled out her checkbook. "I want you to send two chickens to them at once," she said, "and not only today, but every Friday. And three chickens on *erev Yom Tov.* But you must never reveal my identity to them." The butcher happily complied with the benefactress' request and, knowing Mrs. Epstein was a woman of very modest means herself, charged her well below the wholesale price.

But the story doesn't end here. When Mrs. Epstein related her tale, my friend, too, removed a checkbook, anxious to participate in this beautiful mitzva, whereupon Mrs. Epstein added:

"It's funny you should do that because this story actually took place a number of years ago and everyone to whom I've related it has reacted in an identical fashion. *Baruch Hashem*, I now have nineteen families whom I supply with Shabbos chickens, and thank God, countless anonymous people who share my mitzva with me. And all because of my failure to judge my fellow man favorably!"

All too often failures like Mrs. Epstein's do not have such positive results. Our Sages have affirmed that the way one judges his fellow man is the way God will judge him. This, along with the fact that it is a positive commandment from the Torah, should be sufficient incentive to judge others favorably, Inevitably, observance of this mitzva also makes for a happier life.

I have little doubt that *Courtrooms of the Mind* will inspire readers to ask the most frequent questions posed to me regarding all of my books: "Are these stories really true? " The answer, as before, is a qualified "yes."

In the past, by changing the character's names or the stories' locales, I attempted to insure the privacy of those concerned. In this book, since the stories involve condemnations and improper thoughts, it was vital to be extremely careful to disguise the identity of the protagonists. I trust that all of the appropriate precautions have been taken. All stylistic and expository liberties were taken either in light of this concern, or to enhance the impact of the lesson.

The stories in this book can be divided into two categories of judging favorably: "between man and man" and "between man and God." Similarly, in Book II, devoted to children, for whom these lessons are equally important, the same pattern has been adopted. I had hoped to include stories regarding judging "between man and himself" — the tragic situation wherein a person fails to judge himself *l'kaf zechus.* Owing to various considerations and sensitivities, however, I was obliged to abandon this idea. Another subject not dealt with (although referred to in the Halachic Foreword) are instances wherein one specifically should not judge favorably. I hope the reader will understand that it was more important to focus on the greater areas of neglect.

In each of my previous books I devoted the Introduction to extolling the value of a story as a means to convey universal lessons and timeless precepts. I hope this point requires no further elaboration. The topic of this book, judging others favorably, needs no such justification. We are all witnesses to the damage caused when we fail to *dan l'kaf zechus.*

How many arguments and disputes, marital problems, neighborhood quarrels and crises of faith could be avoided by heeding the Torah injunction of judging favorably! How many fights and battles could be averted if we would only give others the benefit of the doubt! Being judgmental is not a state or a condition; it is a malaise. And whereas judging favorably may not be a panacea for strife, it is certainly one of the most powerful preventatives.

Man's drive for self-aggrandizement typically entails the belittling of others. In lauding ourselves we accentuate the faults and imperfections of everyone but ourselves. Herein lies the connection between *dan l'kaf zechus* and *hakaras hatov,* two Torah precepts which combat man's vainglorious egotism. Instead of following our natural instincts to condemn others and to praise ourselves, we are commanded to consciously do the precise opposite: judge our fellow man favorably and recognize that our good fortune and achievements are due to the contributions of others.

It is only appropriate, therefore, that I seize this opportunity to enumerate and thank all those who have helped with this particular project and my few other efforts.

The span of time between conception and execution of this book may not break any world records, but it is certainly a personal landmark. I couldn't have accomplished it without the Almighty's bountiful grace, and the help of His earthbound minions. I therefore *hasten* to thank Diane Deena Cohen for her copyediting, Sara Scheller for her cover design, and Isaac Mozeson, Leibel Estrin, Joseph Goldberg and all those anonymous individuals for their respective contributions to this book. A story published many years ago by Rabbi Nissan Mandel was helpful in my rendition of "The Benefactor's Beginning." I am especially grateful to Rabbi Yitzchak Berkovitz for gracing this book with a halachic foreword and epilogue. His words will enable the maximum to be gained from this volume and alert the reader who might otherwise relegate *Courtrooms of the Mind* to the realm of entertaining Jewish literature.

Acknowledgement must be made once again of my seminary students, an insatiable audience when it comes to stories ("*Rabbi Teller, tell us a story!* "), who proved to be the finest sounding board a writer could ever hope to have. (Thank you for all of your other help as well!) The professionals at New York City Publishing Company are richly deserving of plaudits. I can never thank their operations manager, Mr. Refael Suarez, enough, for the time and concern he has devoted to my books.

I also wish to express my appreciation to those who have helped me personally. I begin with my dear parents and continue to my *Rebbeim* past and present, especially the Mirrer *Rosh Yeshiva,* in whose *kollel* I learn. I must single out several *Gaonim* whose personal imprint upon me has been so profound over the past few years that it can be readily discerned (I hope) in every page of this volume: Maran HaRav Shlomo Zalman Auerbach, Rav Yosef Zeinvert, Rav Avigdor Nebenzahl, and Rav Dovid Hersh Meyer.

Since the publication of *Once Upon a Soul* some three years ago numerous changes, for the better, have occurred in my life. Those who have helped and directed me had only my interests in mind and I am forever grateful. No one has provided more professional encouragement and sagacious advice than my *Rebbe*-in-writing, Marsi Tabak.

The distance between authorship and public speaking is spanned by a narrow bridge. Some prodded me while others towed me across the tempestuous waters; to all I am extremely indebted. It has been my extraordinary good fortune to have been taken under the wing of one of Jewry's most dynamic and benevolent leaders, Rabbi Jay Marcus. I am likewise grateful to Rabbi Baruch Taub for his assistance and direction.

I know of no resident of Jerusalem besides myself who receives so much from some of the finest people in the borough of Brooklyn. Rabbis Dovid Cohen, Shlomo Teichman and Avraham Greenberg; Rabbi and Mrs. Dov Goldbaum and Mr. and Mrs. Avraham Frank are my gracious benefactors.

For Mr. and Mrs. Benjy Brecher a mere *Yasher Koach* cannot suffice. I hope the day will come when I can begin to repay all that you have done for me.

The noblest soul I know from the Soul Series days is also my best defense attorney — and prosecutor — when necessary. She watches over the courtroom of our home and, thanks to her, our children are imbued with the ideals and concepts reflected in these stories הניחו לה, הניחו לה ששלי... שלה היא.

לו יהי וספרי זה יצלח להמעיט מחלוקת בינותנו. לו יהי! יהא זה שכרינו, שאף קב"ה ידיננו לכף זכות.

Hanoch Teller
Jerusalem ת"ו
24 Mar Cheshvan / November 1987

Halachic Foreword by Rabbi Yitzchak Berkovitz

בצדק תשפט עמיתך ויקרא י"ט ט"ו
שנצטוו הדיינים להשוות בעלי הריב, כלומר שלא יכבד הדיין א' מבעלי הדין יותר מן האחר...
ועוד יש בכלל מצוה זו שראוי לכל אדם לדון את חבירו לכף זכות ולא יפרש מעשיו ודבריו אלא לטוב.
ספר החינוך מצוה רל"ה

"With fairness shall you judge your people."
(Vayikra XIX.15)

"The Judges are commanded to deal evenly with the litigants and not recognize one more than the other... Also included in this commandment is that it is right for every man to judge his friend favorably and interpret his deeds and words only for the better."
(*Sefer Hachinuch* 235)

The human being, with his mortal eyes and limited scope of understanding, has been entrusted by the Creator with the God-like task of passing judgment on that which lies beyond the confines of his own self.

Even more novel than the directive of how to judge the actions of our fellow man is the instruction "תשפוט עמיתך — judge your People" altogether: every man is in a position to consider evaluating the acts of others.

The Torah teaches that to be alive is to choose: to be aware and discerning, to recognize good from evil, and only then to choose life. The laws of judgment and admonishing directly precede that piercing declaration and cardinal precept, "Love your neighbor as yourself," to make it clear that true concern, caring, and involvement with others calls for us to be perceptive and discriminating. The Torah's directive is to judge your fellow man בצדק (justly). Not with mercy, not with piety; only with justice; the very same justice necessary for the courtroom. This is clearly indicated by the fact that the source for "justice" in *beis din* is the identical source for how to judge in interpersonal relationships. The courtrooms of the mind may not be any less fair than their legal counterparts.

Interestingly, the commandment to judge others favorably is explained as the requirement to interpret the actions of one's fellow man positively. This would appear to deviate from being rational and objective.

As is the case in all areas of Torah study, it is only by examining the halachic details in depth that we can arrive at the proper insight for comprehending the principles. Source material on this particular commandment includes *Rabbeinu*

Yona, in both *Pirke Avos* and *Shaarei Teshuva,* and *Rambam* on *Pirke Avos* — all explained carefully in the introduction of *Chafetz Chaim,* and dealt with in his laws of *Lashon Hara.*

Our credentials[1] for passing absolute judgment are limited to people we are familiar with. Nevertheless, it is considered a proper attitude to view strangers with a positive eye. It is just this situation that Rabbi Yehoshua ben Pr'chya is referring to in *Pirke Avos,* in saying "הוי דן את כל האדם לכף זכות" make it your practice to judge every man favorably." [2]

The actions of our acquaintances may be seen against the background of their usual behavior, allowing us to see the larger picture and clearing the way for a valid evaluation. An action taken out of context can be only misinterpreted. The nature of the characters as well as their history are inseparable from the story itself.

When the question involves a Torah-observant individual who simply does not usually do the kind of things he appears to have just done, then Halacha declares that our sight is impaired. He did not act improperly! [3] Should there be absolutely no explanation for the act witnessed other than sin, we must assume that it was an

1. רמב״ם ורבינו יונה אבות פרק א׳ משנה ו׳ ועי׳ ח״ח פתיחה עשין ג׳ בבאר מ״ח.

2. ברמב״ם שם סוף משנה ו׳ מדוייק דבאינו מכירו וכף חובה מכרעת יותר אין אפי׳ מדת חסידות לדונו לכף זכות.

3. רמב״ם שם, ״...ראוי שתקח אותו שהוא טוב אחר שיש שום צד אפשרות להיותו טוב ואין מותר לך לחשדו״.

accident, an oversight or, barring any other rationalization, an isolated incident totally out of character that was immediately regretted and shall not be repeated.[4]

If the person in question has an ongoing history of outright evil, then we have no reason to take even his good deeds seriously. A *rasha* has disenfranchised himself from any positive consideration. His "mitzvos" are to deceive, or are otherwise non-altruistic. Of him, *Shlomo Hamelech,* the wisest of men, writes (*Mishlei* 26:25). "כי יחנן קולו אל תאמן בו כי שבע תועבות בלבו" — When he speaks gracefully do not trust him, for there are seven abominations in his heart." [5]

In between these two extremes is the *bainoni*: he doesn't want to do the wrong thing, but it isn't easy for him. He tries — win some, lose some. He doesn't usually eat those questionable goodies — but they sure are tempting! He firmly believes in refraining from speaking *lashon hara,* and really doesn't talk negatively about *most* of the people he knows. If you run into him doing something doubtful, with a fifty-fifty chance that he's doing the wrong thing, e.g. the kosher imitation is a perfect replica, there's just no way of telling. Therefore, what right do you have to assume anything but that this man is enjoying a *glatt kosher* snack, or is otherwise behaving in accordance with Halacha? In such an instance the

4. ר״ם ור״י שם ובח״ח הל׳ לה״ר כלל ד׳ סוף הל׳ ד׳.

5. כ״ז ברמב״ם ורבינו יונה שם.

Torah forbids doubts altogether.[6] And if it's not so "fifty-fifty," if the culprit has that "caught red-handed look" written all over his face, can you still really be sure? Halacha requires that you tell yourself "could be," and nothing more.[7]

Tzeddek means fairness, it also means being realistic. Both are the Torah's conception of justice.

Belief in the Torah requires the performance of all of its commandments, not forced piety that your "insides" never really believe in. The essential message, of course, is to be fair, give your neighbor a chance! You know all too well your own struggles — he deserves the very same kind of understanding.[8]

Hanoch Teller has created an inspiring and most enlightening workbook for broadening our horizons and giving us more grounds for

6. שם.

7. שע״ת לרבינו יונה שער ג׳ מאמר ריח. והנה הח״ח כלל ג׳ לה״ר ה״ז פסק דנכון מאד שיהיה הדבר אצלו כמו ספק ובבאר מ״ח הסביר שכוונת ר״י למדה טובה בעלמא ולא מצד הדין. ועי׳ ר״י באבות שכתב דאפי׳ בנוטה יותר לכף חובה צ׳ לדונו לכף זכות. וע״פ הח״ח הנ״ל ובצירוף מש״כ בפתיחה יצא דמצד הדין מותר לדונו לכף חובה אלא דנכון מאד שיהי׳ אצלו כמו ספק ומדת חסידות לדונו לכף זכות.

8. ראיתי להזכיר כאן מה שדייק ידי״נ הר״ר דניאל ספטנר שליט״א ממעשה באדם אחד שירד מגליל העליון בשבת קכ״ז ע״ב כששאלו במה חשדתני השיבו כל פעם באוקימתא ברורה ושונה עד שבסוף מחוסר ברירה הגיע לשמא הקדיש כל נכסיו לשמים — מכאן דכדי להחשב דן חבירו לכף זכות באמת, לא יצא בזה שחושב, מסתמא יש לו איזה חשבון, אלא חייב להמציא הסבר ברור וסביר לתרץ מעשה חבירו.

objectivity. More cases than our instincts will allow us to consider are barely "fifty-fifty." More people around us than we might readily admit are actually purer inside than out. Sit back and enjoy another "Teller Thriller" and give the brighter muscles of your heart some exercise as you begin guessing the endings. Allow your insides to uproot that involuntary reflex of jumping to narrow-based conclusions. Be fair!

Yitzchak Berkovitz

Reserve judgement

ואם הוא מן הבינונים אשר יזהרו מן החטא ופעמים יכשלו בו אם הספק שקול צריך להטות הספק ולהכריעו לכף זכות כמו שארז״ל הדן את חבירו לכף זכות המקום ידינהו לכף זכות והוא נכנס בכלל מאמרו יתברך בצדק תשפוט עמיתך

חפץ חיים כלל ג:ז

If a bainoni *(one who is generally cautious in his mitzva observance) committed an act that appears as blameworthy as it does meritorious, you must judge this individual favorably as our Rabbis have taught, "As you judge your fellow man, thus will you be judged from Above." This is included in the Torah command, "Judge your People justly."*

Chafetz Chaim Klall 3:7

Just Desserts

JUDGING BY Shneur Haberfeld's *payos*, long black coat and halting English, one would never guess that he is a camping goods wholesaler. How a devout Brooklyn resident ever got involved in this line of work is something that mystifies neighbors and Boy Scout leaders alike. But whether or not Shneur ever donned a backpack, business, *Baruch Hashem*, was booming.

The nature of his work often took him out of his native Williamsburg, and so he sported a sturdy, handsome Oldsmobile. Somewhat of a car-safety aficionado, he had his model equipped with several special features, such as reinforced fenders and security doors. The *Tefillas Haderech* on the dashboard was self-installed. At least once a week Shneur clocked several hundred miles on his odometer by driving to the Catskill or Pocono Mountains to promote his goods and consult with his salesmen.

One crisp spring morning Shneur was preparing for an overnight trip to the Poconos. He had appointments arranged with the directors of several large summer camps and the projected sales were too high to entrust to his salesmen.

Besides fueling up his fancy Olds on trips like this, Shneur invariably treated himself to a sumptuous restaurant meal before setting off. Nevertheless his concerned wife, afraid that even a splurge at a local eatery could never satiate his ravenous appetite, always prepared some hefty *tzaida laderech* bagged food and bottled drink.

ON THIS PARTICULAR MORNING, Shneur saw that he was running late and was afraid he would jeopardize his treasured "pit stop." He therefore pulled up to Goodstein's, the fastest — and fanciest — restaurant in all of Williamsburg. "Ahh Goodstein's," Shneur inhaled into his robust lungs, its very proximity triggering a Pavlovian reaction. The camping goods wholesaler jumped out of his car and practically tripped over a beggar who was camouflaged in the filth of the gutter. The *shnorrer* reflexively extended an empty palm, claiming that he hadn't eaten in days. From his gaunt appearance it didn't look as if he was exaggerating very much.

In a burst of natural magnanimity, Shneur invited the indigent man into the restaurant to share a meal with him. Emphatically and resolutely the beggar refused; yet Shneur persisted.

For close to five minutes he tried to allay the man's fears that customers would not object to his entering such an expensive establishment. Not to be dissuaded, Shneur wrapped his arm around the beggar, revealing a gold cuff-linked sleeve, and gently walked him to the portals of Goodstein's.

"My friend," he assured in a Yiddish as rich as his demeanor, "I am a regular customer here and they love when I come with a guest. Actually it's been a while since I've been here so I'm sure they will be especially cordial."

But for all of his salespitch, the *shnorrer* still demurred. Shneur was running out of patience, and worse, he was running out of time. Still, he felt that he had no right to abandon this man whom Providence had placed in his path.

Suddenly, to the exhilaration of his host, the *shnorrer* acquiesced.

"You know, I'm as poor as a shul mouse," the beggar smiled, "and I could use a good meal."

ELATED, Shneur marched into the restaurant shlepping the *shnorrer* at his side. The eyes of the proprietress lit up when generous Shneur Haberfeld entered. His appetite, budget, and manner of tipping were a restaurant owner's dream.

Shneur gallantly swept his arm over the impressive display of dishes on the counter and offered, "Pick whatever you want; it is my pleasure and my treat." The *shnorrer*'s eyes dilated to their full capacity. He had never seen so much food before.

He stared at the sweetbread, and then eyed the chopped liver. He looked longingly at the *p'chaw* and practically swooned at the endless array of kugels. Shneur, anxious to get on with the ordering, tried to expedite the proceedings.

"My friend, what will it be?"

The beggar interrupted him in a condescending tone: "You may refer to me as Reb Nochum."

"I... I... I'm sorry, *Reb* Nochum," Shneur continued a bit startled, "I understand your hesitation. Decisions like these are always frustrating, but I must head off soon. Why don't you pick out a few dishes, and I'll ask the cook to have small portions of each one placed on a platter. This way you won't feel as if you're missing out on anything."

But Nochum, oblivious to his host's entreaty, moved on to the next group of selections. He tapped his finger indecisively on the glass counter above the kishka, and Shneur, after some initial vacillations, duly arrived at the point of exasperation.

"Just make up your mind already!" the nervous businessman blurted out, attracting the attention of those seated in the restaurant.

THE PROPRIETRESS, realizing that the problem was one of choice, scurried over to point out the most expensive dishes. Shneur smiled weakly, effectively dismissing her. He was immediately full of remorse over his outburst to his guest; his lateness, coupled with his mounting hunger, had made him act impulsively.

Anxiously wishing to make up for the hurt he may have caused his guest, Shneur struck upon an idea. "My friend, uh... er, Reb Nochum, I mean," he offered in a mollifying, complaisant tone, "I see that you are having a hard time making up your mind. Perhaps you are afraid that you will order something too expensive and then feel ashamed that I am eating a simpler dish. You have my solemn word that no matter what you order I will order the exact same thing. How about that, huh?" he added, hoping to prompt the man into a selection.

The *shnorrer* seemed comforted by Shneur's offer and at

last arrived at a decision. "Fair enough," he responded and proudly pointed... to the compote.

"Ye... yes... fine. Good choice, but what about the main dish?" Shneur pried involuntarily. By this point his own appetite seemed to be placing the words directly into his mouth.

"No, no, that will be it," Nochum replied with a glow of satisfaction radiating from his face. He folded his arms across his chest, waiting for his host to place the order.

"Are you *sure*?" Shneur urged, in as mild a voice as he could muster, his growling stomach making him regret his commitment to the man.

"Oh yes," Nochum responded triumphantly.

WITH SHOULDERS SLUMPED, Shneur shamefacedly shuffled over to the counter to place his order of "two compotes." A broad smile adorned the lady behind the counter as the defeated philanthropist approached.

"Meester Haberfeld," she greeted him warmly, "a pleasure! You want maybe the Weiner Schnitzel with side order Tzimmes and Mamaligge, as usual? Or maybe the Hungarian Goulash with Palachinka? Or maybe just a nice, plain piece Boiled Flanken, I'll throw in Potato Knish or Kasha Varnishkes no extra charge."

"No," he replied barely audibly. "Two compotes."

"Two com... WHAT?!" she shrieked, unable to believe her ears.

"That's it," he whispered apologetically.

She glared at him with utter astonishment, which quickly

degenerated into derision.

"All right," she cried, "if that is what the man wants, that's what the man gets!" and stomped off into the kitchen.

"You *hear* this?!" the proprietress declaimed to the kitchen help.

Everyone heard her. They heard her across the street. They heard her down the block. *They heard her across the bridge.* "Meester Haberfeld doesn't trust my *kashrus* now. A *guest* he brings me, looks like he hasn't seen food since *erev Yom Kippur*, and then has the gall to shame me in front of all my customers! Two compotes! *Two compotes* he orders. You hear what I'm saying! A menu a *poretz* would give half his land for, and this Haberfeld — you should excuse me, a businessman — picks the boiled fruit. A *chutzpah!*

"Baila," she fumed and muttered under her breath, slamming pots, pans and meat cleavers on the stainless steel counter tops, "give the big businessman and his guest their boiled fruit. Put in glass bowls, better — for all I know he won't eat off my china either."

COMPOTE WAS SERVED, but as far as Shneur Haberfeld was concerned, he was eating humble pie. He just couldn't figure it out. How could a starving beggar, who by his own admission hadn't eaten in days, pass up such an opportunity: all-you-can-eat in a *fleishig* restaurant?!

For once Shneur was genuinely grateful that his wife had insisted on preparing provisions for the trip. He wolfed down the compote, thanked his guest for the company, and in his haste forgot to leave a tip on the table.

The proprietress was livid, Shneur was starving, the

shnorrer was delighted, and the other customers were dumbstruck.

Shneur made his way through the afternoon traffic, madly munching on every carrot stick, potato latke and oatmeal cookie he could fish out of the large bag on his lap. He crossed the Williamsburg Bridge onto the FDR Drive, up to the GWB and over to New Jersey, stuffing himself and mulling over the morning's events.

HE WAS ALREADY ON ROUTE 209 north near the Delaware Water Gap when a horrible sight filled his rearview mirror. Six high school drivers engaged in a game of "chicken" were approaching at breakneck speed. Chicken was a game that had no winners, and safety-conscious Shneur feared that just by virtue of being on the same highway, he would be embroiled in this battle of wits and guts.

Leading the pack was a little orange coupe, followed by a Nova that tried to take the lead on the curve. The other four cars closed in, and one of them leaped ahead of the rest, just missing Shneur on his right. The Brooklyn wholesaler caught a glimpse of the acne-faced driver and winced.

The boy's fat, red face looked like a doughball, and his pouty lips were skinned back from his teeth in a rictus of fear. The kid gripped the wheel as tightly as he could, smart enough to keep his power on while he used light brake.

The back left wheel, however, lost its traction on the asphalt, and the tail of the car whipped toward the side, kicking up a storm of dust and stones as the rear wheels went off the road. The car seemed to hang there for a moment, and then, with its wheels churning, the tread caught and it shot out of the skid toward the opposite side of the road. The driver didn't manage to cut his speed fast enough and he spun half-around before being struck head-on by the little orange coupe. Like a bull trying to gore a fallen matador, the coupe seemed to lower its head before performing a headstand and vaulting over the spinning car, coming down with a force that shook the highway bed.

The Nova tried to pull to the outside, power on. But Shneur, desperate to avoid the accident, was trying the same thing at the same time, and there wasn't room for two. The cars tangled and there was a heavy price to pay. The Nova rammed into the high guardrail, tearing loose a long chunk of metal boilerplate. Its driver bobbed inside his car like a white cork as the machine twisted away from the fence and rolled over and over. Shneur was thrown toward the inside and smashed into the overturned coupe.

Meanwhile three other cars came braying, screaming and snarling down the stretch. They swerved like mad to bypass the crash, but one Camarro lost a wheel. Its axle dug into the highway, making it end-over-end like a shot bird in a crippled flight. It finally flopped down, sliding along the cruel tar bottom-side-up, grinding and mashing blood and guts. The air was redolent with burning gas, oil, rubber and metal.

It didn't take long for the state troopers and emergency personnel to arrive at the scene. Miraculously Shneur had fared much better than the other drivers caught in the accident: he was only in shock. The camping wholesaler's predilection for safety had not been in vain. The triage EMT was relieved by his condition and assigned him the lowest priority for treatment.

"AT LEAST WE could look at this guy, without... well, you know what I mean," said the young state trooper to the medic who was attending to Shneur. "He ain't even got no cuts and bruises. Can we get a statement from him?"

"Not so fast, Smokey," the medic shot back. "If he doesn't come to soon, his blood pressure will continue to drop."

"What's that you're giving him, smelling salts?" asked the officer.

"Stroudsburg Medical Center is a little more sophisticated than that. Why don't you do your job and keep these rubberneckers away?"

The closest "rubbernecker" was adorned with *payos*. "Excuse me!" waved Refoel Leibowitz, armed with a thermos and some Tupperware.

"Look here, Doc," said the trooper. "It's another one of them Jew Amish. Maybe they're brothers, or maybe he's got a formula to say in Jew language that will snap this guy out of his shock."

THE MEDIC LOOKED UP with interest and beckoned for Leibowitz to advance. "You know more than you think, Smokey." Speaking louder for both the trooper and the chassid to hear, he added, "Perhaps this gentleman will provide some familiar, reassuring stimuli. I can't have you shaking the poor guy for your accident report. He has to come out of it slowly." The trooper stepped away from the dazed wholesaler and gave the floor to Leibowitz, the fortyish proprietor of the area's only kosher hotel.

"*Shulem Aleichem*," opened Leibowitz; "I pulled over when I saw a policeman helping a Yid out of that smashed-up car. I'm sure you'll be *bentching gomel* over this one."

Shneur didn't respond and kept looking straight at nothing. The medic began to prepare a hypodermic, while the trooper was scribbling the words "unable to report at this time."

Leibowitz unscrewed the thermos and announced, "Iced tea. It's still cold."

Shneur didn't budge.

"And what do we have in here?" continued the hotelier, snapping open a Tupperware bowl while trying to sound cheerful. "Aahh, I see it's only a *shtickel* compote."

Shneur's eyes grew large as the compote flashed red from the light of a half-dozen ambulances and police cars. "Com... com... compote, compote," he stammered, looking around him as though a blindfold had just been lifted. "Of course, the compote! I thought the *shnorrer* was making fun of me, and the owner thought we were making fun of her. Then I thought that the *shnorrer* was angry at me for not giving him money for schnapps. But no... he was just a poor, hungry man. And smart enough not to eat veal or goulash on an empty stomach. No, he was a humble fellow. He was genuinely uncomfortable there, and I, I shouldn't have pushed so hard and been so judgemental. Now I realize that in the merit of helping Reb Nochum, I'm still alive."

"Go on," said Leibowitz, pretending he knew what in heaven the man was talking about.

"I know, now I know," repeated Shneur, fairly flinging the Tupperware bowl onto the Interstate, "never to condemn someone for appearing ungrateful..."

Heard from: Rabbi Hillel David

Alone

IT'S HARD TO SAY if Dr. Rappaport is a naturally exuberant individual. His constant, toothy smile and jovial demeanor are part and parcel of his work. His reputation as one of Jerusalem's finest and most respected pediatricians emanates from his medical prowess, while his popularity derives from his concern and friendliness. When asked how he is able to maintain so cheerful an outlook with a hectic practice such as his, he shrugs and explains that *someone* has to look cheerful in an office always crowded with chicken-pocked children and bawling babies. But for all of Dr. Rappaport's congeniality, he was not about to brighten Rivkie Shreiber's Wednesday morning.

Rivkie was the consummate, Brooklyn-born and bred wife of a *kollel* fellow: gregarious, endearing, wide-eyed, a touch flamboyant — in short, very American-*frum*. But beneath the façade of stylish wig and fashionable attire beat the faint heart of a timid Bais Yaakov graduate terrified to be on unfamiliar turf. A newcomer to Israel, Rivkie did not have local family or close friends, and barely spoke the language. The little biblical and mishnaic Hebrew she could muster evoked gales of laughter from the natives. To have found a pediatrician who was not only well-qualified but able and willing to speak to her in her own tongue was a relief.

As Dr. Rappaport's deft fingers examined Rivkie's seven-month-old baby Deena, however, his smile faded. This was not the common ear infection or simple case of bronchitis for which a standard prescription and best wishes for a *refuah sheleimah* would suffice. The baby's chronic listlessness and soaring temperature were the symptoms that alerted him; stool specimen tests corroborated his tentative diagnosis. There was little doubt now as to the nature of Deena's ailment.

As gently as he could, Dr. Rappaport broke the news. His diagnosis etched painfully sharp lines in Rivkie's brow, reducing her vivaciousness to stony silence. She had never heard of shigellosis before, but she had known that her Deena wasn't suffering from an ordinary case of diarrhea.

To make sure that the baby received the proper care, Dr. Rappaport told Rivkie the truth: "This disease can be fatal in infants. It is also highly contagious. The baby must be admitted to a hospital immediately."

"FATAL?!" Rivkie thought to herself, her heart pounding loudly in her ears. "Oh, my God!" Her hands trembled as she attempted to button up Deena's creeper. If this simple chore of closing a button seemed a near impossibility to her now, how in the world was she supposed to manage to bring Deena to the hospital? Besides being nearly hysterical with fright over her baby's condition, Rivkie could barely breathe at the prospect of all the red tape that would surely confront her there. She often became flustered and embarrassed when attempting minor transactions at the bank or supermarket; how, then, could she battle the infamous *bureaucratzia* to admit her baby into an Israeli hospital?!

Rivkie's thoughts drifted back to the more carefree times of her childhood, when her warm, large family was always there to help her over even the most inconsequential hurdles. Tears welled up in her eyes as she recalled her mother's kind, loving face. But Rivkie's daydream lasted only a split second; her maternal instincts catalyzed her into action, burning through the inertia of despair. This was no time to sob on the phone to Mommy in Brooklyn. She had to take care of Deena herself, and she had to act *now*.

Reaching down into herself for the fortitude she *had* to have, she turned to the doctor and said: "Tell me exactly what I must do."

"I am preparing all of the papers," he told her while he quickly tended to a veritable ream of printed forms. Dr. Rappaport punctiliously explained each item, repeating himself where he thought it was necessary. He then escorted mother and child out of his office, ensuring that the infectious baby did not come into contact with the dozen patients in his waiting room.

ONCE OUTSIDE, however, Rivkie's courage waned. Of all the times to be left on her own! Her husband had flown to the States the night before for his brother's wedding. Even before the present crisis, she had felt incompetent dealing with the normal rigors of daily existence without her husband's patience, calmness and fluency in Hebrew. She had never been so completely alone before.

Rivkie had come to Israel for the same reason many of her peers had: she wanted her husband to ascend in learning, and "*ain Torah k'Toras Eretz Yisrael.*" Attaining that goal entailed a sacrifice on her part in terms of separation from family and friends, but she was sure it was worth it. Besides, it was sort of a tradition. Hadn't Rabbi Akiva's wife, and all of the wives of *talmidei chachamim* before and after her, made sacrifices for Torah's sake?

Because of budgetary considerations, Rivkie had not traveled with her husband, but she no longer regretted having remained behind. The thought of toxins attacking her baby in mid-flight with no proper medical attention available was even worse than the current state of affairs, as bad as it was.

RIVKIE RACED THROUGH HER APARTMENT, stuffing into a bag whatever she thought Deena would need in the hospital. Just when time was so critical she found everything disorganized and nothing in its place! Frantically scurrying from the baby's room to hers, she improvised, settling for anything that was clean and serviceable. She snatched the *sheitel* off her head and put a *tichel* on in its place, knowing intuitively that she would be in for a long, draining ordeal where looking her best was the lowest priority. She grabbed pajamas for Deena and a denim skirt for herself, as her fingers fumbled for the *Tehillim* on the shelf below her husband's *shas*. Grasping the little book she reassured herself, "I'm not really alone," in an effort to fight off the terrible thought that Deena might never return to their apartment.

To complicate matters, one of the pediatrician's forms had to be stamped by the *Kupat Cholim** office in downtown Jerusalem before Deena could be admitted by the hospital. Rivkie's few encounters with *Kupat Cholim* led her to fear a protracted process involving several offices and interminable lines. But even if it were to go quickly this time, how could she take Deena with her? On the other hand, how could she leave her very sick and contagious baby with a sitter or a neighbor? The walls of her apartment seemed to be closing in on her. There were no doors in sight.

Rivkie's instincts impelled her to get the baby to a hospital without delay. If necessary, she would turn on the charm and hope for the best. If a womanly approach failed to get her any medical attention, she would... she would... she'd just scream!

RIVKIE DIALED FOR A TAXI and explained that it was urgent. But the problem with taxis is that *every* caller feigns urgency, desperation, or the like in order to receive a cab in a reasonable amount of time. Waiting for a taxi at any time is a trial of patience; waiting for one in an emergency is a test of nerves. Rivkie failed both.

But the mother was not the worse off. While Rivkie and her daughter were waiting for the cab to arrive, Deena began to convulse. Her fingers kept clenching and unclenching. Her eyes rolled wildly and she hissed through her closed mouth. Rivkie clutched her baby tightly in her arms, her eyes darting up and down the street frantically. Just then the taxi pulled up at the curb.

* "Sick Fund," medical insurance program.

As they sped away, Rivkie implored the cabbie to drive as quickly as possible. She nearly screamed each time he slowed down for another red light. Her body tightened like a spring around her baby's twisted form, and she prayed that the hospital would soon be in sight...

DEENA'S GRAVE CONDITION circumvented the admission procedure. When the taxi finally arrived, it went straight to the emergency room entrance. Layers of red tape fell away when the medical staff saw the agonized baby and her panic-stricken mother.

The convulsion passed but its effects lingered. The insidious toxins attacking Deena's brain had turned her into a baby her mother couldn't recognize. An alert attendant in the ward sized up the situation at once and rushed to notify a doctor. Within seconds Deena was injected with a tranquilizer.

The baby was placed in a crib, and a medical team huddled around. One nurse inserted an IV tube into Deena's wrist, while another left to arrange a spinal tap and a third took her blood pressure. The doctors prepared a stool sample and ordered a battery of other tests.

Rivkie was unable to comprehend the Hebrew words flying back and forth, but the word "*shigella*" cut into practically every sentence. "What's happening with my baby?" she pleaded several times, but the doctors were too intent on their work to respond. They motioned for a nurse to remove her so that they could continue unhampered.

"Not to vorry," a nurse tried to assure Rivkie in broken English, "you baby go upstair to qvarantine and get good care." Not worry?! Rivkie was terrified! The doctors' looks of concern and the pediatrician's earlier warning about fatality converged like cymbals crashing in her ears. She trembled and began to cry hysterically.

Rivkie loved her baby more than anything in the world, and the thought of her demise was... God forbid! She refused to allow that unimaginable thought in her head; it was too horrible even to contemplate. The death of a child was the kind of tragedy no one ever thought could befall his or her own family; it only struck hapless strangers and was only discussed in dark whispers that hovered somewhere between sympathy, shock and *lashon hara*.

It was amazing that in just a few short months one could grow from a teenaged *kallah* into a mother willing to endure the worst tortures ever conceived in order to save her child. Rivkie would have gladly changed places with little Deena if only to spare the baby just a second of pain. She chastised herself for having earlier indulged in homesick thoughts of Brooklyn, and wasting precious seconds — seconds that might have meant the difference between life and death.

As helpless as she felt, Rivkie was determined to do anything to save her Deena. But for the time being her lonely crib-side vigil, constant *tefillos*, and continuous loving caresses were all she had to offer.

AT SIX FORTY-FIVE in the evening Deena was moved from the emergency room to the Quarantine Section of the Pediatrics Pavilion. It had been eleven hours since Rivkie had last eaten, but she was still too inexperienced to know that in order to tend to her baby properly she had to take care of herself as well. It was so hard to be separated from Deena, even for the few minutes she would have needed to find some food. Feeling as alien and vulnerable as she did, Rivkie instinctively sensed a hostile environment. Even though she knew that the hospital housed a professional, caring staff, Rivkie felt an evil presence lurking in the corridors. Dizzy from hunger and fatigue, and consumed with anxiety over her daughter, she was unable to think rationally.

As the attendant wheeled Deena's crib out of the elevator, Rivkie's worst fears were realized: from the corner of her eye she suddenly caught sight of a hideous black monster. A gasping shriek escaped her lips and she fell upon her baby to protect her from the creature's sinister gaze.

"What is that?" she whispered urgently, but the attendant, a cold, seasoned hospital worker, neither replied nor flinched. He continued to push the crib, dragging the stumbling, histrionic mother along.

"Wait, wait, please!" Rivkie begged as Deena was wheeled straight toward the monster. Frantically tugging at the crib to prevent the attendant from advancing, she alarmed the whole floor. "Can't you hear me?" she yelled. "Please, let's go the other way. Can't we go the other way?" Nurses and patients rushed to the scene of the commotion and began to jabber in Hebrew about the crazy American. A nurse tried to get her to let go of the crib and calm down, but it was no use. A security guard was called.

RIVKIE THOUGHT she was living a nightmare. The spasmodically twitching monster, emitting a fetor as foul as the stench of a charnel house, was advancing closer and closer, and everyone was conspiring to bring Deena into his vile clutches. "Help! HELP ME!" she screamed. But her pleas fell on deaf ears.

The security guard arrived and first set about dispersing those who had gathered to watch the spectacle. He and the attendant exchanged a knowing look. Then, approaching Rivkie from behind, he grasped her arms and removed her bodily from the path of the crib. Rivkie struggled to wriggle free, but she was no match for this burly, experienced guard.

Devastated, Rivkie watched helplessly as Deena was wheeled inexorably closer and closer toward the monster. How could they do this to her baby? Clearly the beast sensed another victim approaching. It raised its massive head, displaying gruesome, bloated lips that opened and closed like the mouth of a giant fish. Rivkie moaned, and the guard tightened his grip. She felt faint, but she forced herself to maintain consciousness. She had stumbled into a nightmare world: this was some voodoo temple behind the façade of a hospital. Before her very eyes, her baby was about to become a heinous sacrifice on the altar of a hideous god. The crib was nearing the monster, which raised itself on its elbows in anticipation, a white froth forming around its distorted lips. Rivkie's breath caught in her throat as her eyes bulged out of their sockets. She had no voice left to scream.

When the attendant came within the creature's reach, it thrust out a blackened limb to arrest the advance of the crib. But miracle of miracles, the attendant waved it off and continued into the pavilion. Rivkie started to breathe again. Deena was safe from this *bête noire* for the moment... but who knew what perils awaited her inside? The guard released her at last, and Rivkie ran after her baby.

But as she approached the frightful miscreation, it once again extended a ghoulish black limb. She leaped out of its reach, racing to catch sight of the attendant pushing Deena's crib into a private room. A nurse was busy taping a sign to the door — *Highly Contagious.*

Rivkie had almost forgotten her earlier hellish encounter,

attributing it to nerves and exhaustion. But as she dropped off to sleep, she again found herself face to face with the frightening monstrosity she had seen in the corridor a few hours before. In her dream he was standing over her, trying to pull Deena from her arms. His black talons ripped her daughter away and carried her toward a raging fire. With arms raised, he held the little body above the flames, ready to hurl her into a fiery furnace. Rivkie shrieked uncontrollably, waking herself and baby Deena. It took some moments before she was able to restore both the child and herself to normal. And even then, alone in the dark, all her fears resurfaced. Was she safe from his vile clutches here in this ward? She could not shake the haunting feelings that he had aroused in her.

SHIGELLOSIS, Rivkie soon learned, is a disease not quickly cured. The nerve-racking experience of a prolonged stay in the hospital was somewhat ameliorated by the slow but steady improvement in Deena's condition. After a few days the baby's temperature dropped and she appeared less sickly. The diarrhea, however, did not relent.

On the fourth day, Rivkie detected some difficulty in Deena's breathing. Her observation was confirmed by a doctor, who quickly ordered a chest x-ray.

Alarmed by the new development, Rivkie escorted Deena down to the radiology department. When they emerged from the elevator the terror of that first night was abruptly rekindled. Propped up in a bed, only meters away, was the same jet-black beast, his face indiscernible but for the opening and closing of gruesomely swollen, protruding lips.

Rivkie flinched involuntarily and tried to prevent herself

from again emitting a terrified shriek. She instinctively threw her hands around Deena to shield her from the gaze of the creature and kept her own eyes riveted to her daughter.

After a few brisk strides Rivkie realized, to her profound horror, that they were headed directly into the path of the dreadful beast. She had begun to hyperventilate in fear. What could she do? She turned sharply and walked backwards, pretending the attendant needed her to help pull the crib.

Suddenly she felt a hand brush her back and Rivkie jumped as if stung by a live wire. She was too petrified even to scream. She ran, pulling the crib all the way back down the corridor to their room.

He had touched her, there was no doubt about it. She felt that she immediately had to have her blouse incinerated. What *mikve* was wide and deep enough to cleanse her of the contamination of that demonic contact? Was it the Satan that had grazed her, or the Angel of Death? Rivkie was shaking and sobbing, gagging from terror.

The attendant caught up with Rivkie and threw her an angry look. He grabbed the crib and deliberately began pushing it back toward Radiology. Rivkie simply could not believe how nonchalant the hospital staff was about that most ugly of creatures! Surely that thing should be kept away from good, healthy people. Didn't they realize that God would not punish one so unless he truly deserved it? She couldn't imagine what sin could be so iniquitous that Hashem would mete out such a punishment.

THE X-RAY TECHNICIAN asked for her help in placing the baby on the x-ray table. Rivkie froze, afraid to touch her precious Deena. Who knew what pernicious disease could possibly be transmitted by contact with that Frankenstein? The technician let out an exasperated sigh and repeated his request through clenched teeth. With a sudden shock, Rivkie realized that *her* child was the contagious one on this floor, and she had no time to worry about whether *she* had contracted some horrible disease from the monster. She'd have to save her own personal worries for that silent hour of the night when subconscious thoughts invade the conscious mind, robbing the soul of sleep.

The head radiologist examined the x-ray of Deena's chest and scribbled some notes. Everything was in order and they prepared to return to the ward. Rivkie begged the attendant to tell her if "it" was still in the corridor. He informed her with a smirk that *he* had been moved, and she prayed that the man was telling the truth. Rivkie had heard that hospital workers become inured to everything, but that accursed creature's condition was far worse than any debilitating disease or chronic ailment she could ever imagine. She was still frightened, and couldn't expel the horrible visage from her memory.

RIVKIE WAS QUIVERING FROM HEAD TO TOE from the experience, which no one had bothered to explain to her. After seeing it at close range, she now understood that the "monster" of her hysterical imagination was actually a pathetic human being with some unspeakable disease or congenital defect. Surely the mark of Cain had not been as pronounced, she thought, and wondered what abominable sin this person must have committed to have deserved such a frightful disfigurement. She hoped she would never know. Rivkie prayed that she would never see it again and that she would be able to erase the memories of this harrowing day. She needed to concentrate now on her baby, she tried to tell herself, not on the few moments of horror with that malevolent creature. But the image of the monster made her shiver suddenly and violently. It somehow embodied all of her fears, everything she couldn't face.

LATER THAT NIGHT, a nurse brought Rivkie a cot so that she could sleep alongside her daughter for the night. Her presence was needed to change the diapers that Deena was soiling with such frightening frequency. She also had to notify the nurse when the intravenous solution ran out, since they paid less attention than normal to the quarantined patients.

Rivkie collapsed on the cot, a little more in control of herself after the quick meal she had practically inhaled while standing over Deena's crib. Her thoughts drifted to her husband, Yossie. His brother's wedding was to take place tonight, she recalled. Tears swam in her eyes as she visualized all the happy, smiling faces of friends and relatives who would be dancing with the bride and groom... while her baby was here in this sterile, unfriendly hospital, hovering between life and death.

How Rivkie had wanted to join Yossie on his trip home! But in the end, she herself had decided to remain in Jerusalem, knowing full well that they could scarcely afford a second plane fare. Her parents had been generous enough when Deena was born, and Yossie's parents were already strapped with all the "extras" a wedding calls for. The thought of being alone in a foreign country had been daunting, but she had not dared to tell him for fear of spoiling his trip. Now she wondered what she could possibly have done to have brought this torment on herself and little Deena.

Rivkie glanced down at her baby. Deena was looking so much better, thank God. But what use was her recovery if this monster would cast some satanic spell upon her? If ever there was an "evil eye," it was his to give.

Because Deena was kept in isolation, Rivkie didn't have the opportunity to discuss the matter with other patients or visitors to the hospital. The next morning, she told herself, she would bring up the problem with Deena's doctors. Rivkie had no intention of asking for a history or medical analysis of that poor soul's condition: she simpy wanted to know how they could allow such a thing to remain in plain sight — roaming all over the hospital and terrorizing patients and any sane visitor.

BUT THE OPPORTUNITY NEVER AROSE. The next morning a physician came to visit Deena, flanked by interns and residents. He turned to Rivkie and said in near-perfect English: "I have good news for you. Your daughter is showing real improvement. She's making a far more rapid recovery than we had anticipated considering her condition when she was first admitted to the hospital. I imagine she will have to remain here for another day or two — pending examination by the head of Pediatrics. He will probably put your daughter on phenobarbital tranquilizers for several months, and, as a matter of course, order an EEG six weeks after discharge to see if the convulsion has left any lasting effects."

The doctor's "good news" didn't sound all that cheery to Rivkie. Aside from the part about leaving the hospital soon, the prospect of an EEG made her fearful once again. Then the nagging, subliminal question that had been haunting her every night came to the surface:

"Will my daughter have any brain damage because of the convulsion?"

The doctor tried to allay her fears: "Electroencephalograms are performed routinely on anyone who has experienced a convulsion. Undoubtedly in your baby's case it was a *shigella* toxin that caused the seizure, but we just want to make sure she doesn't have a tendency to convulse - data which would be very valuable for you to know."

The thought of being released from the hospital was blissful - but it was marred by the nightmares and the overwhelming stress Rivkie had suffered from her grisly encounters with the ubiquitous monster. Who knew what ghastly scars this experience would leave on her and the baby?

THE NEXT MORNING the department head examined Deena as promised, and announced that she could be released that day if lab results corroborated his prognosis. Needless to say, Rivkie was elated when the lab gave Deena the green light; the dreadful week in the hospital would soon be over. Rivkie had to go downstairs to handle the paperwork before the release could be authorized — a procedure that took close to an hour.

When she returned to Deena's room she found a nurse getting the baby dressed to leave. "Well, you're all set to go," she cheerfully greeted Rivkie. The nurse was British, the first native English-speaker Rivkie had met all week. "Submit a copy of the papers you received downstairs to the nurses' station near the entrance to this ward, dear, and you'll be on your way. Oh, yes, I also have a message for you: Yigal wants to say goodbye."

"Yigal?"

"Yes, you'll find him at the desk."

Rivkie wondered who Yigal was. Maybe he was the intern who had received them in the emergency room and had come up several times to check on Deena's progress. Or perhaps he was the taxi driver who had driven them to the hospital and who had refused payment — that first day and again when Rivkie subsequently met him near the outpatient clinic.

Rivkie packed their few belongings, picked Deena up and turned to the nurses to thank them for their care. Each glorious step was bringing them closer to freedom. She was finally leaving, just in time to get ready for Yossie's return in only two more days. She would need that time to get the house back in order and put this whole ordeal in proper perspective. What was she supposed to have learned from it?

RIVKIE APPROACHED THE NURSES' STATION and began kissing Deena's forehead excitedly while she waited for someone's attention. Deena's lively personality had been almost fully restored and she babbled merry gibberish while her mother *kvelled.*

A nurse finally turned to them, and Rivkie handed over the mass of papers. After a brief perusal, the nurse said she needed the passport numbers of both Deena's parents. Rivkie smiled and reached for the purse she had placed on the counter — and nearly jumped out of her skin.

There he was, looking directly at her from down the corridor! "Oh dear God," she whimpered. "Not now, when we are almost out! Please, just let us leave this place!" She clutched Deena tightly, pressing the baby's head into her side. Deena struggled to wriggle away but her mother refused to relax her grip.

"*Nu?*" demanded the nurse, rolling her eyes. "I... I don't... know," Rivkie spluttered back. "I... I must go now, and I will call in the information."

"Wait just a minute," the nurse replied sharply, "I must ask the head nurse." The nurse got up and went into the head nurse's office. Rivkie remained frozen in place, her eyes tightly closed. She didn't know what to do. She wanted to run away, but was afraid they might call downstairs and not let her out of the building. Without an official release from the ward she would be ineligible for reimbursement of both the hospital fees and the cost of the EEG, which the head of the department had said was so crucial. She was trapped, a captive victim of his vile gaze. She began to tremble once more, her earlier elation forgotten.

"Mrs. Shreiber... Mrs. Shreiber?"

She was being spoken to. "Yes," she answered, startled, and opened her eyes.

"Do you have at least *one* of your passport numbers with you?" the head nurse asked. She was a middle-aged woman with an air of efficiency about her, and she appeared more cooperative than the nurse who had gone to get her.

"Uh, uh... yes, sure."

"Then that will be adequate. Now, if you don't mind my saying so, your baby appears to be very uncomfortable. It seems you're crushing her! Are you trying to conceal something?"

Rivkie realized how foolish she must have looked, but she was scared, scared for herself and for poor Deena. She and her baby had gone through enough. She did not need to look at the monstrous face of sin in the form of a man.

BUT WHY WAS EVERYONE ELSE so calm about his presence? Irony of ironies, *she* looked like the queer one, and "it" was treated like a cherished patient to be wheeled around, deposited wherever he wished, and tolerated throughout the hospital by one and all.

Grabbing hold of herself, Rivkie reached out again for her purse. This time she saw that he was inching closer to her and, to her consternation and utter chagrin, she let out a high-pitched, long-surpressed screech.

"What's the matter?" the head nurse asked in alarm.

"N... nothing," Rivkie responded, controlling herself. She fumbled for her passport and hastily read off the number. The nurse jotted down the information and nodded her approval.

The last hurdle was behind her now, and Rivkie could finally leave. As the nurse stamped the document and handed it back, she told Rivkie that Yigal was waiting for her, and would she just take a few more minutes of her time to speak with him?

With all of the tension, Rivkie had completely forgotten about the mysterious Yigal. With the monster so close she did not wish to remain an extra second. But who was this Yigal?

"Please tell him that I'll call him," Rivkie said hurriedly, "but I don't remember exactly who he is."

"You don't know who Yigal is?" the nurse asked with surprise, as though Rivkie had not recognized the name of the Prime Minister. "Why, he is lying right at your side!"

Rivkie cowered. "What *is* he?" she asked, ashamed that her tone evinced such disgust.

"What *is* he?" the nurse repeated in bewilderment. "Yigal is our favorite patient, that's who he is."

AT THIS POINT Rivkie's anger overcame her fear. "Favorite patient? How dare you all treat him like some privileged character when obviously he's a living example of the wrath of God!"

The nurse was about to respond when her superior interrupted. "Why don't you ask him yourself how he got to be this way? Go ahead," she cajoled, "he's waiting for you. He has wanted to talk to you for some time now."

Rivkie, her anger spent, became flustered and stared pointedly at the counter. She felt faint again, and wished she were somewhere, anywhere but in the company of that malfeasant.

In the meantime the head nurse wheeled Yigal right over to her. Remembering the interdiction of the Rabbis forbidding one to look an evil person in the face, Rivkie felt no urge to violate the rule at this time. Close up, she was certain, his features would be even more gruesome than they had appeared from a distance.

The hiked, ballooned lips parted and the creature uttered a muffled "Shalom."

"This young lady," the head nurse told Yigal, "would like to know how you came to look like this."

"*Motek*," Yigal mouthed laboriously, "for my buddies I would be willing to burn a hundred times, just so that Jewish boys might be saved."

All this time, Rivkie had not shifted her gaze from the counter. But when she heard these last words about saving

Jewish boys, she lowered her eyes to the foot of Yigal's bed. Deena had fallen asleep and Rivkie supported her on her shoulder.

"Go on, Yigal," coaxed the head nurse, "tell her your story." A few people in the hallway gathered around him.

"IT WAS THE FIRST DAY OF THE WAR," he began in such surprisingly perfect English that he might have been a foreign correspondent, "Operation Peace for Galilee, that is, when we set out. We were part of the armored brigade which was to lead the attack on the western axis up the coastal road. Almost all the boys in my unit were *Hesder* yeshiva students, just eighteen- to twenty-year-old conscripts who were seeing action for the first time.

"We had regrouped within Major Haddad's enclave in Lebanese territory, and at 11:00 A.M. we headed out for the U.N. zone.

"Half an hour after starting out, shells began erupting. From a fortified position on the road to Tyre, Palestinian terrorists showered the lead tanks with a hail of rocket-propelled grenades, but it didn't take us long to destroy their position.

"Just a little while later those same lead tanks were blown off the road when our own planes mistakenly bombed the crossroads just as we were approaching. Fortunately our tanks sustained only minor damage.

"Since the directive was to reach the Kasmiye bridge over the Litani River as fast as possible, the lead tank unit did not engage in any mopping-up operations after we destroyed the Palestinian stronghold. This enabled them to regroup before the advance of the second unit.

"The problem was that the commander of the paratroop battalion farther back in the column was unfamiliar with the area, not having been briefed as fully as we had been. To compound the problem, his communication system became inoperative just as his armored personnel carrier crossed the border.

"The battalion mistakenly traveled through citrus groves. This made visual contact very difficult for us, while it allowed the terrorists easy access to the battalion. From out of nowhere, RPGs were fired and several tanks and APCs suffered direct hits. My unit was trapped.

"We were being hit from all sides and lost contact with our commander. Soldiers started leaping out of their disabled vehicles before they exploded, frantically running for cover in all different directions. Several, including our commander, were captured by the enemy.

"I also had to bail out of my APC; the steering mechanism had been jammed by a rocket. I was painfully aware of the fact that many of my buddies could not escape from their vehicles. A little ahead of me I saw a Merkava tank get hit and burst into flames.

"The rear escape hatch was engulfed in fire and I knew that the tank's crew was roasting inside. I pried open the door and crawled in to save my comrades. My clothes were on fire."

BY NOW EVEN MORE PEOPLE had congregated around Rivkie and Yigal. They urged him to continue as he paused to catch his breath.

"I found the entire crew alive," Yigal rasped, "but they were unable to extricate themselves from their positions. I pulled and shoved with all my might to maneuver them toward the escape hatch. The door at the end was still burning, but once you were out you could roll on the ground to extinguish the fire. The tank's gunner was in shock and bleeding badly but we even managed to push him out. Thank God, those boys are all fine today."

"And you, Yigal? What happened to you?" asked an orderly who had heard the story many times but never ceased to be amazed by it.

"By the time I was able to escape, the chute was red-hot. My skin melted right off of me. Most of it remained on the walls of the slide." He paused, dropped his head, then added with renewed animation, "But I'm telling you, *chabibi*, if I could have, I would have gone into a dozen such tanks — anything to save our boys!"

Yigal fell silent. There were tears coursing down his own charred cheeks, and his damaged hands were shaking.

RIVKIE HAD BEEN CRYING for some time now. So these stories *did* happen to real people, not just to nameless faces you read about in the *Jerusalem Post*. *These* were the valiant individuals who risked their lives to save fellow Jews, men who fought and suffered the most horrible disfigurements so that women like her — and infants like Deena — could live safely in the Land. Heroes, she realized with a sense of profound shame, weren't the child-women who braved a stay in a hospital for a few days.

How she had incriminated this courageous man, accusing him in her mind of terrible deeds! She had been so involved in her own troubles she had failed to consider *his* possible sorrows. She had shunned and castigated a fellow Jew based on nothing but her own fears and weaknesses. How could she ever make up for the pain she had inflicted, the untold suffering she had heaped on him?

"Please," Yigal said, speaking directly to her now, "forgive me for frightening you. You see, I sometimes forget how I must look to others. When I saw you with your sick little baby, all alone and so worried, I wanted to comfort you. I, too, would love to have a family, a home, someone to care — *really* care — about me. But the truth is, I have no one. I've been here so long that even my old comrades have tired of visiting me. So I live through others, experiencing the pain and the joy of people here in the hospital. It's become a sort of hobby for me. Believe me, I only wanted to help you. Instead, I scared you. I forget how ugly I must look. Please, please," he said softly, "I've been wanting to ask your forgiveness."

Rivkie looked deeply into Yigal's moist brown eyes. "*Ashrecha*, Yigal," she began through her tears, "*halevai* there should be more like you among our People."

AFTER A FEW PARTING WORDS, Rivkie Shreiber finally left the hospital, but she knew the ugly scars would remain on her *neshama* for some time, a small reminder and a meager price to pay for her unpardonable act of misjudgement. She stood on the sidewalk a moment and inhaled the crisp, fresh air of Jerusalem. The streets were awash with sunlight.

Rivkie stared out the window of the bus all the way home, her thoughts in turmoil. "As soon as we get home," she told her precious sleeping baby, "I'll bake him a cake. And tomorrow I'll bring it to him — can you imagine, no one visits him?" She smiled to herself, thinking how happy it would make Yigal to have company.

All at once, Rivkie felt buoyant, lighthearted. One small scar had suddenly disappeared.

Heard from: Aidel Teller

Framed

ANY COMPREHENSIVE LIST of the most acclaimed artists of the '80s would have to include Raquel Stein near the top. In just one year Raquel Stein retrospectives graced the galleries of the Philadelphia Museum of Art, Washington's Hirshhorn Museum and London's Tate Gallery, ranking among the most comprehensive one-man shows ever assembled. Every showing received tumultuous accolades from critics representing different facets of the art world: trade magazines, galleries, and auction houses.

Not since the time of the legendary Edwin Landseer had an artist managed to combine Victorian gloss with such tearjerking lucidity. The curving contours of the Renaissance school combined with the spectrum of brilliant colors attributed to the Impressionist school projected an idealized realism never quite captured before with such resplendent consistency.

Like her mentor Landseer, whose extraordinarily

realistic representations of fur, fin and feather made him a demigod of popular culture, Stein also focused on animals, especially dogs. In one way, she actually surpassed Landseer in that she added a softness to her paint, a feminine touch of velvet.

It was a touch that tugged at the heart and brought tears to the eyes. A touch that communicated love and innocence in a way which wasn't as much viewed from the outside as it was felt from within.

Projecting ideas about social hierarchy and decorum onto animals — partly to satirize human behavior, but mainly to suggest that the divisions of society are rooted in a natural order — Stein provided a new perspective on the canine, and thus the human, condition.

Art may be the ape of nature, but dogs are the apes of human morality. Canines have a tendency to reflect the better aspects of mankind: friendliness, fidelity, tenacity, bravery, and gentleness. Raquel conveyed each doggy eye moistly reflecting those traits. She stroked as much moral pathos into the amber eye of a hound as the Victorian painters etched in their renditions of the last act of *Romeo and Juliet*.

Stein's anthropopathic prowess extended to every detail of her subjects, so that an Alsatian's glossy, well-groomed coat and erect posture simulated the self-acclaimed rigidity of habit so common amongst European gentry. These unique abilities resulted in an unprecedented "artburst" of excitement for anything associated with this patron saint of Landseer devotees.

MYSTERIOUSLY, at the peak of her career, when everything she laid her brush to was exhibition-quality and pricey, Raquel Stein vanished! She left no forwarding address, no letter to her friends and fans, no reason for her disappearance.

Gone were the furry faces peering out of doghouses, and lazy cocker spaniels stretching out in the morning sun; no more leaping Labradors or oodles of poodles frolicking in the grass. Obviously, her absence did not remain unnoticed for very long.

Rumor had it that she had repaired to a kennel for a sabbatical to observe more closely the idiosyncrasies of the canine kingdom. But the rumor was wrong.

Actually, what happened is that Raquel discovered that while art could mimic life, it couldn't give it meaning. After a great deal of internal searching, she began to look for a religious identity. Her quest began with Judaism and never went any further. Unwittingly at first, Raquel discovered in mitzva observance a purpose and significance that she had never known before. Furthermore, she concluded that the inspiration behind her painting was Divine in its essence. Raquel sincerely believed that the observance of Judaism would enhance and insure the continuation of that inspiration.

BECOMING RELIGIOUS was not a facile endeavor for her. She began visiting Orthodox families in Brooklyn, and was drawn to their warmth and spiritual fervor. Gradually she found their lifestyle as irresistible as it was formidable. Her mind told her that a religious commitment meant abandoning a successful career just when everything was going her way. She imagined herself married, with ten kids in a small apartment and a *shmatte* on her head.

Her heart told her that her ritzy suite, exclusive

restaurants and glamorous friends were not making her a better person, or a wiser one. She became obsessed with the thought that if she were truly interested in living a productive, meaningful life, then she should live as an observant Jew, the way her grandparents did, and their parents before them.

Privately, discussing it with no one, Raquel began to read, to study, and eventually to learn. After she became observant she understood that there was only one place for her to live: Israel, the land of her heritage.

RAQUEL EXCHANGED the world of art and money for the world of Torah and mitzvos. She purchased a studio apartment in the Makor Baruch section of Jerusalem and rechanneled all of her artistic drive into her new love of Torah Judaism. She spent her time attending a seminary for women, and found her previous craving for prestige and glory repugnant. She had had her fill of the limelight and now preferred a life of modesty.

When word of her new-found passion reached the ears of her closest friends, they reeled in disbelief. They set out to find her and persuade her to convalesce during a protracted rest on the Italian Riviera — anything that might restore her to her senses!

But removed from the art milieu and engrossed in the world of Torah observance, Raquel never felt so sane. She understood that God had endowed her with an exceptional talent for a purpose. It was up to her to discover how to harness it in the service of God.

In the beginning, Raquel restricted her painting to works of leisure, requiring little emotional involvement. It then took on a more cathartic role, as she worked out the conflicts that tag along and nag anyone who has exchanged the mundane for the holy. Finally, painting became an economic necessity, as she painfully realized that her savings were running out.

What she didn't realize was that she was about to undergo a crisis, a kind of test to determine her very fate and future, not as an artist, but as an observant Jew.

IT ALL STARTED INNOCENTLY ENOUGH. Every few weeks she would produce a painting and take it to a local frame shop not far from her apartment. The owners, Aviva and Ophir Regev, followed her detailed instructions to the letter. After all, it wasn't often one got a customer who was both talented and steady.

One day Raquel, who now preferred the Hebrew "Rochel," brought in two paintings to be framed. She was running low on money and expected these works to improve her financial situation.

"Please take special care of these," she nervously requested. "They're to cover my living expenses for the next few months."

"I will do my best. You can stop by in about two weeks," Ophir replied.

As Rochel stepped out of the frame shop and onto the sidewalk, she halted and remembered that she had forgotten to get a receipt. A little voice inside her said, "You really don't know the owners. If you don't get a receipt, you could be asking for trouble!" In a moment she summarily dismissed the idea as silly, a form of paranoia that affects artists who put much time and effort into a work and then put that creation into the hands of a stranger.

WHEN SHE RETURNED two weeks later to pick up her paintings, Rochel gingerly opened the brown paper wrapping to inspect her work. She saw the first painting surrounded by a golden frame that played against a green matting. "Good, good," she thought, "but where's the second one?

"It's not here!" she yelled involuntarily.

"What's not here?" asked Aviva.

"My painting! You know, the painting of the collies. Where is it?"

"You must have made some mistake. You only gave us one painting."

"I did not. I gave you two! I know I did."

"Please, calm down, and let me see your receipt."

"I don't have a receipt! Your husband didn't give me one."

"My husband isn't here right now. But if you'll have a little *savlanut*, he should be here in just a few minutes."

In Israel, a "few minutes" falls within the parameters of half an hour and forty years. Usually Rochel took it in stride, but not this time. The high stakes made it the longest twenty-minute wait of her life.

Ophir finally arrived. He took a few more puffs on his cigarette, savoring a few more moments of leisure, before stepping into the room that served as the Regevs' gallery and reception area. He gave a friendly wave to Rochel but did not notice the anxiety permeating her countenance, for he was immediately addressed by his wife.

"Ophir, did you see this lady's painting? She says she

brought in two, but there's only one here and she doesn't have a receipt."

"I don't remember a second one. Are you sure?" Ophir asked Rochel patiently.

"Of course I'm sure! It *must* be here!" she snapped back.

"If you left it, I would have remembered framing it. Now, please, look at home. You probably misplaced it."

"Me? Why are you placing the blame on me? I brought two paintings in here. And you took them!"

"Listen, take your painting and go home. I'm sure the other one will eventually turn up," he said condescendingly.

"I'm not taking one painting, I'm taking two. And you better find the missing one before I come back!" she threatened. Despair hampered her ability to protest further. Rochel quickly turned and stormed out of the shop empty-handed, slamming the door behind her.

A DEJECTED ROCHEL STEIN paced back and forth in her apartment. Wave after wave of anxiety and frustration relentlessly attacked her imagination, and she began to suspect the worst.

"It must be that they saw a chance to cheat me. I'm sure they sold my painting. That explains why they didn't give me a receipt. But why did it have to happen now, when I'm almost broke? Why did they appear so honest before?"

Rochel picked up the phone to call the police and then hung it back up. "They would never believe me without a receipt. A *dati* American against two Sabras. Forget it."

Her mind began to review the past eighteen months. "Maybe I should quit being religious, give everything up and go back to the world I knew best. At least there I knew who the hustlers were! This is Israel, for Heaven's sake, and Israel is supposed to be different!"

Thought after thought cascaded through her mind, charging and gathering momentum with each passing minute. She desperately looked for a way to stop, to slow down.

ALL OF A SUDDEN an idea, like a celestial phone call, rang in her head and she rushed to pick up the receiver. "There is a mitzva," Rochel said to herself with as much resolve as she could muster, "to be *dan l'kaf zechus* — to judge favorably." She sat down in a chair and determined not get up from her seat until she could think of some *zechus* that would prevent her from mentally incriminating the Regevs.

She contemplated and reflected, but her mind refused to comply. The circumstantial evidence coupled with the shock of having actually lost her painting blocked any creative thought in this direction. But Rochel's artistic nature finally came to the rescue. Her ability to see things with a keener eye than others, to view from a multifaceted perspective, provided her with an idea.

"Judging favorably means that there must have been an innocent mistake. They must have accidentally framed both paintings together!" she decided at last. At first the idea sounded utterly absurd: even an amateur framer wouldn't make such an error. But the more she thought about it the more she was convinced that this was the explanation.

Rochel triumphantly got up from her seat and left for the frame shop, assured that she would find her lost painting stuck to the one they had shown her. Every stride she took toward the store reinforced the idea in her head.

Yet when she arrived, she became fainthearted and no longer trusted her resolve. She had only the courage to suggest a thorough search.

"I'm sure the second picture is here," she begged Ophir and Aviva. "Please, please let me look around."

"If you wish," Aviva responded coldly. "But if my husband says we don't have it, then we don't have it."

Now it was Rochel's turn to be cold and methodical. Print by print, frame by frame, she worked her way through the store. By the time she reached the last ten framed pieces, her heart had sunk to her shoes.

"It *must* be here!" she told herself. But it wasn't. By default she reverted to "Plan A"; it was her last and, by this time, her only hope.

"Could I please see my painting?" Rochel asked firmly, without alluding to all of her wasted effort in the last forty-five minutes.

Her painting was silently placed on the counter. "I would like you to please open the frame," she requested politely.

By this time, the Regevs were both sure that Rochel was trying to lure them into some kind of trick. Ophir spoke up: "If you think that once I open this frame you can just take your painting and have it framed elsewhere without paying me, you're mistaken."

"Just open it," Rochel insisted. The atmosphere in the store thickened. Rochel could feel her shoulders tense up. "Judge favorably," she kept repeating inwardly.

OPHIR TURNED to get his knife, his pliers, and his screwdriver. "I have warned you," he said before he meticulously inserted the blade. He then undid the screw which held the hanging wire and pulled apart the nails on the edges of the frame. With deliberate precision, he reinserted his knife, running it along the paper backing.

The wooden border holding Rochel's stretched canvas fell softly onto the counter.

Rochel took her canvas from him, fiddled with it a bit... breathed a sigh of relief, and smiled. The two paintings were stuck together to make one!

"*Baruch Hashem*!" she said gratefully.

"Why... why... how did... how could it happen? How did you know?" Ophir asked, with a mixture of embarrassment, shock and surprise.

"The Torah tells us to judge others favorably," she replied, "and I tried to fulfill the mitzva. Yet there seemed to be so much against it. At first, you didn't give me a receipt. Next you denied seeing my second painting. Then I couldn't find it.

"I was nonetheless obligated to come up with an ethical explanation to absolve us both of blame. In the end, this was the only possible solution, as crazy as it sounded.

"I was taught that judging favorably isn't really crazy; most of the time the truth shines through. Now all you have to do is tell me how much I owe you for the framing, and I shall be on my way."

Both Ophir and Aviva were stunned into silence during this recitation. When they finally succeeded in finding their tongues, the new respect and admiration they had for

Rochel and her commitment to living by the mitzvos inspired them to observe and to tell others about this important commandment of *dan l'kaf zechus.*

Heard from: Rebbetzin Yehudis Samet

As you judge

❦

אם הוא רואה אדם שדיבר דבר או עשה מעשה בין ממה שבין אדם למקום או ממה שבין אדם לחבירו ויש לשפוט דברו ומעשהו לצד הטוב ולצד הזכות אם האיש ההוא ירא א־לקים נתחייב לדון אותו לכ״ז אפילו אם הדבר קרוב ונוטה אצל הדעת יותר לכ״ח

חפץ חיים כלל ג:ז

In the realm of either "between man and God" or "between man and man" you are obliged to judge a God-fearing individual's speech and actions favorably, even if they appear improper.

Chafetz Chaim Klall 3:7

Rabbinical Supervision

ASK A CONGREGANT what his rabbi does and, after a few scratches of the head, thoughtful rubs at the chin, and a little hemming and hawing, he may suggest that the cleric gives a weekly sermon and occasionally performs some "other official stuff." Ask a rebbetzin like Malka Fleishman and she would heave a weighty sigh, spread her palms to her hips in mock indignation and say, "*Halevai* the Rabbi could sit and cultivate his *kavod* like some uptown emeritus. Then I might even get to see my husband a few times a week!" For in addition to delivering the weekly sermon and "other official stuff," her Rabbi performs weddings and funerals, decides halachic matters, and adjudicates disputes; and very likely, if not for his tireless activities the congregation — and perhaps the shul building itself — would collapse in a heap.

Apparently, tradition sides with the Rebbetzin's view. The rabbinical appellations *klei kodesh* (holy vessels) and *oskim betzorchei tzibbur b'emunah* (those involved in the community's needs in faith) are meant to connote more than merely a "speech *zugger*" who lectures on the weekend.

Naturally, the larger the Jewish community, the more qualified should be the individual selected to fill the role of spiritual leader. It goes without saying, therefore, that the most distinguished Jewish community on America's eastern seaboard — outside of New York — would settle for nothing less than an outstanding, God-fearing scholar to become its rabbi.

Its choice was Rabbi Shmuel Fleishman, who, at the age of thirty-four, had already earned an unparalleled reputation in Europe as a learned, inspiring leader. As it happened, their selection fortunately spared the Rabbi and his family from the Nazi inferno. Altruism, authoritative decision making, exemplary conduct and dauntless leadership were among the meaningful ways Rabbi Fleishman repaid his host community.

By the 1950s and '60s his fame had spread far and wide in North America, and offers for ever more prestigious positions poured in, yet he viewed as his sole obligation those who had sponsored his family's escape. He fulfilled his job with selfless dedication, and part of his self-imposed rabbinic responsibilities included bimonthly trips to New York to arrange the supply of communal needs such as kosher meat and *esrogim,* to interview candidates for local positions, and to meet with other prominent rabbis regarding national — and occasionally international — matters of importance for the Jewish People.

IN 1961, about two decades before the introduction of the high-velocity AMTRAK metroliner, such a journey was a six-hour excursion making every local stop, and then some, along the way. In order to create the minimum inconvenience to the community, Rabbi Fleishman routinely traveled on the night train, which departed for New York before midnight.

The train ride, SRO with jobbers, nocturnal boulevardiers, and assorted insomniacs, could never be construed as a viable alternative to bed rest. The cacophony of the conductor's incessant announcements of upcoming stations, coupled with the din of idle conversation, clashed with the numerous wall posters, which pictured a gentleman in a gray flannel suit calmly snoozing in what appeared to be a quiet, empty car. "Enjoy a Tranquil Ride" read the caption.

Nonetheless, the Rabbi did find a modicum of relaxation in these journeys. For two nights a month he received no phone calls, heard no late knock at his door, and was not besieged by a flurry of *shailos*.

One crisp spring morning the train pulled into Manhattan's Pennsylvania Station to the conductor's cry of "Last Stop, New York City!" Rabbi Fleishman grabbed his satchel and, with a benediction of gratitude on his lips, hoisted his journey-stiffened limbs onto the platform.

That year Rabbi Fleishman was saying *Kaddish*, and he was in a hurry to get to a nearby shul in time for an early *minyan*. Yet even at 5:30 in the morning the Rabbi found himself awash in a sea of humanity, commuter waves breaking in all different directions.

NEW YORK CITY is the one place in America, indeed one of the only places in the world, where 5:30 AM is as bustling as other cities at peak rush hour. The area around Penn Station is as busy as... as, well, Grand Central. Located just two blocks west of Herald Square, Penn Station is in the heart of the garment center. During the course of the morning alone, more than a million commuters and workers pass within a ten-block radius of the terminal. Small wonder that every hour of the clock is astir with activity.

These fifty thousand legions of feet are fueled by the Big Apple's incomparably vast array of fast-food outlets. Developed to an exact science, these emporia can serve an order of burger, fries, and Coke in a matter of milliseconds. Thousands of trays full of soggy bacon and eggs, watery juice, and rancid coffee slide across counters and down gullets in 99-cent breakfast specials that are hardly breakfasts and not very special.

State-of-the-art fast-food joints are also designed to allure the maximum number of customers. For this reason the storefronts, invariably composed of solid glass, display incentives and inducements that are further reflected off the interior mirrored panels. The net result is that customers with rapidly moving jaws are visible to the hordes passing by outside.

What better point-of-purchase advertising can there be than dozens of 3D executives consuming fresh-from-the-oven doughnuts or steaming slices of pizza without even placing their attaché cases on the counter? And what is more "New York" than a business lunch composed of munching a hot dog while haggling on a pay phone?

PERHAPS THE KOSHER JEW is the only one not tempted by the plethora of instant gastronomical gratifications available on every block. Still, it doesn't mean that he is oblivious to these happenings.

Rabbi Fleishman was no exception. For the most part, the endless stream of customers crowding each restaurant were no more than an amorphous blur. But when he passed a Nedick's on the south side of the station his eyes suddenly focused upon a sight that made him stop dead in his tracks. Thus frozen by the scene, the Rabbi posed a hazard to several unwary commuters, who proceeded to slam into Penn Station's sole stationary being.

Sitting on the first stool in Nedick's was a most distinguished member of his community. More than just the main *gabbai*, this man often represented the congregation at the *amud*, conveying the *kehillah*'s prayers to the Master of the Universe.

Rabbi Fleishman did not want to believe his eyes. Yankel Helfman was the very one who supervised the catering in the shul. How many times did fish, fowl and meat pass from Helfman's trusted hands to the Rabbi's own mouth?!

And there sat Helfman, center stage, framed by a row of fluorescent strip-lighting in the orange and green interior. He was hunched over his tray eating God knows what with desperate abandon!

THE SIGHT was appalling. Here was one of the Rabbi's most respected congregants eating "*glatt treif*" with total impunity. Obviously the man was convinced that no one he knew would possibly see him so far from home and so early in the morning. Suddenly Rabbi Fleishman saw a flashback of when Helfman — juice and cookies in hand — ran out of the *sukkah*. "Has he no fear of God?" the Rabbi questioned indignantly, deciding at once to strip this fellow of all communal responsibilities. Anger gave way to betrayal, despair, and eventually a sense of personal failure.

In a moment, the Rabbi regained his composure.

"What right," he asked himself, "do I have to judge Helfman unfavorably? The Torah requires us to judge everyone favorably, except a *rasha*. Although this act does appear to involve a wanton *aveirah*, I must nevertheless think of some plausible reason for his action." The Rabbi's talmudic mind began scanning formulae, edicts, and responsa with a frantic urgency.

"An ulcer, that's it, an ulcer!" Rabbi Fleishman cried aloud. "It must be that Helfman has an ulcer and had to eat and drink immediately. If one doesn't eat immediately in such a situation it could seriously endanger his life."

Fortunately Rabbi Fleishman had the advantage with which Torah scholars of his caliber are blessed: granite-like faith. "If," he reasoned, "judging favorably is what the Almighty has commanded us to do, then I am obliged not merely to *believe* in Helfman's innocence, I must be *convinced* of it! This explanation vindicates him; thus any confrontation, even a tactful one, could embarrass Helfman deeply."

Before Helfman could look up and notice, Rabbi Fleishman continued briskly on his way. The Rabbi determined not to give credence to any excuse other than the one he had just concocted.

But it wasn't easy. His inner voice chastised him for being ridiculously naive. He was simply covering up: covering for Helfman, and, worse still, for his own failure as a Rav. Yet he fought and struggled to hold on to his conviction.

OVER THE NEXT several days the Rabbi kept his promise to himself and did not confront Yankel with the incident. However, when Helfman placed some sliced turkey on his plate during a festive *kiddush* in the shul's downstairs reception hall, Rabbi Fleishman winced involuntarily.

But a week later, just when the Rabbi's vicissitudes of thought tipped in favor of approaching the *gabbai*-cum-Nedick's patron, Helfman seemed to be avoiding shul. Inwardly, the Rabbi was relieved.

When, two weeks later, Rabbi Fleishman found himself again in Penn Station — this time to visit members of his community who were hospitalized or recuperating in New York — and he passed the "scene of the crime," he froze in his tracks once more. The very sight of those fluorescent light bulbs framing the corner counter evoked a feeling of nausea. Catching someone you know and trust commit a blatant sin is a feeling akin to indigestable grease settling in the pit of your stomach. The haunting memory was so vivid that it was as if Helfman sat again at the same seat. In his place, however, a doe-eyed black woman sat plumbing the depths of the *Daily News*.

True, the Rabbi had judged Helfman favorably, and conjured up a moderately plausible alibi. Nevertheless, passing the Nedick's once again undermined the opinion he had been determined to retain. Like a persistent gnat, doubt encircled him, buzzing into his ears that Helfman was a *rasha* and repeating that the Rabbi was nothing more than a foolish naif who presided over a congregation of sinners and hypocrites.

D*AN L'KAF ZECHUS* often means ascribing positive intent, and even virtue, to what are reprehensible acts. The Torah actually mandates violating human nature, commanding us not only to judge such situations favorably, but to believe sincerely in that judgement! Rabbi Fleishman abruptly struck his satchel with the flat of his hand, as if dispelling in an instant those demons of doubt. Steadfast in his commitment, the Rabbi marched past Nedick's on his way to the nearby shul.

Later that afternoon Rabbi Fleishman arrived at the NYU Medical Center, the third stop on his hospital route. He walked down the maddeningly identical corridors of the giant complex to visit a congregant currently residing in 11C. White-uniformed personnel padded down hallways redolent with antiseptic.

Rabbi Fleishman pushed open the hydraulic door of 11C and found the appendicitis victim, whose name had been entered into his appointment book by his Rebbetzin while he was sound sleep. He was about to back quietly out of the room when he caught sight of a patient at the opposite end of the ward toying with the IV apparatus attached to his arm. The Rabbi's jaw dropped.

"Oh... Rabbi, Rabbi Fleishman, come in," said Yankel Helfman. "What a pleasant surprise! How did you know I was here?"

The Rabbi's mouth opened to respond, but the shock had reduced him to muteness. He blinked hard several times, assuring himself that his imagination hadn't admitted the *gabbai* to the hospital.

"They tell me the emergency operation was a success... not that I feel so *yontiffdik*, you understand," Helfman added in a tone designed to keep his Rabbi concerned enough to stay awhile.

"The operation...?" the Rabbi asked hesitantly.

"For the ulcer, my bleeding ulcer. Ruchel didn't tell you? You have so many important things on your mind you must have forgotten. I myself was trying to forget that I had this — but what are you laughing at, Rabbi? Not these pajamas, I hope. My Ruchel insisted on bringing..."

"Of course not, Yankel," said the Rabbi, still chuckling with laughter that shook his entire frame. "It's just that this is, uh, the first I hear that it's an ulcer, and, well... frankly I'm relieved. I'm so relieved that it's not something else... eh, something much worse."

THE RABBI pulled over a chair, indicating to his congregant that this was not just one more stop on his *bikkur cholim* list.

"I was a fool for letting my condition get out of hand like this," Helfman said, clutching his generously bandaged midsection as if to emphasize the point. "You shouldn't know how many times in the last two months this thing made me drop everything and grab desperately for the nearest food and drink."

"I shouldn't know..." agreed Rabbi Fleishman.

"Rabbi, you shouldn't know the kinds of places I found myself eating in," he added *sotto voce*, his outstretched hands poignantly demonstrating the helplessness he had known.

"I shouldn't know," smiled the Rabbi, patting the shoulder of his trusted *gabbai*.

Heard from: Rabbi Shimon Schwab

Abstemious Indulgence

THERE ARE THOSE who still recount the magnificence, the opulence and the splendor that reigned in the royal court of Reb Yisrael of Ruzhin.

To thousands of his chassidim, and just as many of his admirers, his royal manner was only fitting for a *tzaddik* such as he. After all, the Ruzhiner, as Reb Yisrael was known, was a man who was looked upon as the conduit, so to speak, between them and God Himself. He had the power to plumb the depths of man's despair and to release the holy sparks of creation at any level. And he was a man who could, if he so desired, reach into Heaven itself and hasten the coming of a reluctant Messiah.

Yet to others, Reb Yisrael's seemingly extravagant lifestyle was seen as a danger, an excess which evoked resentment and opposition, and could ultimately threaten the spread of chassidus.

Imagine: here was a man who appeared to live a life of

unbelievable and undeniable wealth. His huge, handcrafted carriage was drawn by a brace of perfectly matched stallions that not only pulled the carriage, they pranced with it. They were the envy of prince and *poretz* alike. Reb Yisrael's raiments were the finest to be had in all of Europe. The rich, black-brocaded *kapota* was so custom-tailored that it seemed the silkworms had spun their tiny threads around Reb Yisrael's body for a perfect fit.

Another element of Reb Yisrael's apparently "ostentatious" existence provoked public criticism: his boots. Never before had such pomp graced the feet of a Jew. According to some accounts, they were made of the purest gold, with exquisite, baroque carvings. They were the kind of footwear that only the wealthiest of men could afford, and that only a king would boast.

But it was neither the beautiful craftsmanship nor the inestimable value of the material that made these boots truly unique. The uniqueness of these boots, unbeknownst to anyone but their owner, lay in the fact that they had no soles. The very same boots that appeared to the outside world like two golden tributes to the affluence and glory of their owner were in actuality mere façades. In effect, it was as though Reb Yisrael wore no shoes at all!

Reb Yisrael's fleshly feet walked on hard, stony ground. In this way he would not and could not forget that his golden boots, his "*zaidene kapota*" and his magnificent carriage were only the trappings of this world, and by no means its essence.

ONE OF REB YISRAEL'S most outspoken critics was Rabbi Chaim Halberstam, a celebrated rebbe and *talmid chacham* who could not separate the sole from the soul, and opposed the Ruzhiner's lifestyle. Reb Chaim, better known as the Zanzer Rav, criticized certain individuals not for their religious zeal, but for what he thought were their materialistic excesses.

Reb Chaim's brother, Reb Avigdor Halberstam, was the embodiment of both a holy lifestyle and an eschewal of luxury. An adherent of an old, ascetic form of classical Chassidus that had its origins over a century ago among a group of men known as the *perushim* — literally, those who separated themselves — Reb Avigdor was its paradigm. These *perushim* believed that in order to achieve a closeness to God, one had to withdraw from earthly pleasures.

Reb Avigdor's *avodah*, his service to his Creator, was to refine and elevate the three garments of his soul — his thought, his speech and his action — to such a level of pure spirituality that the physical world became insignificant. What did exist was Godliness, pure and simple.

This is not to say that Reb Avigdor ignored the world; it simply did not have any meaning for him. Light and dark, hot and cold, hunger and satiety — all were the same.

Reb Avigdor spent his life wandering and preaching an ascetic way of life. During the course of his travels he often mingled with the local villagers and accepted whatever meager accommodations they were kind enough to offer. Eventually they came to know him, and his reputation as a saintly, purehearted man began to spread.

ONE DAY, he was invited to be the *sandek* for the first son of Reb Michel the *baal agalla* (wagon driver). Reb Michel and his wife, Sheina Brienda, were blessed with six daughters before the Master of the Universe bestowed them with a boy. Perched atop his wagon Reb Michel had witnessed Reb Avigdor's holy ways from near and far and therefore asked the pious *porush* to do him the tremendous honor of being his son's *sandek*. Reb Avigdor agreed.

He cradled the newborn in his arms, and his thoughts concentrated on the mystical significance of *bris milah*. Reb Avigdor watched as Yosel the *mohel* bent over the baby, heard Reb Michel recite the blessing and felt the little baby's body tense up. But his thoughts never wandered from their lofty plateau. In seconds, it was over and the townspeople cried: "MAZEL TOV! MAZEL TOV!"

The beautiful ceremony of *bris milah* was followed by an equally beautiful and bountiful *seudah*. Reb Michel and Sheina Brienda were not wealthy in a monetary sense, but they had a wealth of friends who wished to share in the *simcha* and mitzva.

"Eat... eat, Reb Avigdor. It's a mitzva!" Reb Michel urged his honored guest.

"I'll wash and have a little bread. But please do not be offended if I refrain from partaking of the main course. You realize, of course, that consuming a full plate is not necessarily a sign of a full heart — merely a full stomach!" Thus Reb Avigdor managed once again to spare his host an expense, and at the same time retain his comportment of physical denial.

In the earlier stages of Reb Avigdor's journeys he had traveled alone and actually shunned company. But before long, a devoted group of disciples gravitated to the *porush* and followed him wherever he went.

As his fame spread, Reb Avigdor regularly received invitations to the homes of the more prominent members of the local communities. He often used these opportunities to build a bridge between those who were in a position to give and those who were in a position to receive.

ONE *EREV SHABBOS*, Reb Avigdor and several of his students were invited to spend the Holy Day of Rest at the home of Berke, the grain merchant. Berke was a man of means, observant, generous and, if the truth be known, accustomed to having his own way.

Early Friday afternoon the table was arrayed just the way Berke liked it. The company observed settings of gleaming silver, sparkling crystal, and an exquisite lace tablecloth that was said to have come all the way from Warsaw. With a look of contentment Berke surveyed the scene with his distinguished guests, and then commented in a satisfied tone, "I don't believe that there is anything more beautiful than a Shabbos table..." Suddenly, he stopped in mid-sentence.

"Wait a minute," he shouted, "where are the saltcellars? Masha, get in here right away!"

A slight girl of about fourteen came scurrying out from the kitchen, wiping her work-worn hands on her apron. "Wh... what is the matter?" she stammered timorously. "Did I do something wrong?"

"I told you to set the table!" he said sternly. "You have forgotten the salt!"

"I'm... I'm so... so sorry. I must have been in a hurry to finish making Shabbos."

"Well, see that it doesn't happen again! When my guests and I return from shul, we expect everything to be perfect."

"You must understand," Berke told his guests

apologetically, as the exhausted and obviously despondent girl scuttled back to the kitchen, "she's an orphan. We took her in two years ago. Not very bright, but at least she's a hard worker. I suppose one of these days she'll get married, but in the meantime we keep her here."

Reb Avigdor tried to encourage Berke to be more understanding. "God chose the Jewish People," he explained, "because they were 'the smallest of the nations.' This refers to the ability of the Jew to make himself 'small,' to subjugate his own will to the will of his Maker.

"By taking the poor girl into your home you have done this, but in order to really fulfill the mitzva properly, you have to treat her like one of your own, and that includes giving her the benefit of the doubt. In fact, it's a good idea to get into the habit of judging others favorably, particularly if you yourself wish to be judged this way. Sometimes even a great rabbi may do something that appears to be the opposite of good!"

"Thank you for your words of Torah," Berke countered. "Let me assure you that I treat her just like I treat everyone in my family. I give her clothes, food and a place to stay. And if I demand a lot from her, it's only because I also demand a lot from myself! But enough of this, we're going to be late for shul."

BERKE AND HIS HONORED GUESTS joined the townsfolk in the humble shul. Berke was chosen to lead the congregation and his booming voice and joyous energy brought all those assembled into the Shabbos spirit. Before departing everyone paid tribute to his masterful davening, and calls of "*Gut Shabbos*! *Gut Shabbos*!" echoed throughout the streets.

Reb Avigdor and his disciples slowly made their way to

Berke's home. The darkness outside made the candles inside glow even brighter, and the light leaped and mirrored off the elegant candlesticks, crystal goblets and gleaming silverware. The missing saltcellars had been placed neatly at the head of the table.

After *Kiddush* and *Hamotzi*, Berke graciously invited his guests to partake of the *seudah*. "If anyone leaves this Shabbos table hungry," he exclaimed, "it's his own fault!"

As was his custom, Reb Avigdor ate sparingly.

"Is there anything wrong, Rabbi?" Berke asked. "Why aren't you eating like your colleagues?"

Reb Avigdor smiled. "As you know, sublime thoughts accompanying the actual act of eating are capable of raising the holy sparks found only in food that is kosher. I can tell by the way everyone is enjoying himself that my help isn't needed in this regard."

THE GUESTS continued their meal and the evening passed, bathed in the sweet warmth and glow unique to the Sabbath. It would have been superfluous, and indeed might have detracted from the joy of the Sabbath meal, had mention been made of the incident of Masha and the saltcellars, so the subject was discreetly avoided.

In fact, everything continued to go quite well until Shabbos lunch, when Reb Avigdor did something that evoked a sense of awe, curiosity — and utter amazement.

Berke, his wife, his four children, and his guests were all unusually hungry. It seemed that both the Rabbi's eloquent *drasha* and the *chazzan*'s mellifluous *mussaf* had been delivered in a way expressly designed to impress Reb

Avigdor, and as a result the Shabbos davening lasted much longer than usual. The scent of the simmering cholent that filled the house was more tempting than ever. The challah, as delicious as it was, did little to satisfy everyone's whetted appetite.

"We have a little custom in our house," Berke announced, "to allow a special guest to serve the cholent. Please, Reb Avigdor, do the honors if you will."

Reb Avigdor was about to demur, but the savory cholent was ceremoniously placed before him. He gripped the handles of the pot, intending to pass it to his host, when he smelled the steaming mixture of meat and potatoes. Suddenly, Reb Avigdor stopped. He hauled the cholent back toward his plate, and began sampling it straight from the pot!

"It's really quite good," Reb Avigdor declared. "Very tasty!" At least that's what it sounded like, because frankly it was difficult to understand what he was saying. He kept eating and eating, stuffing overflowing ladlefuls of cholent into his mouth faster than he could swallow them! Chunks of meat and gelatinous globs of potatoes fell into his beard, looking like boulders in a hairy forest. Clusters of beans and other unidentifiable ingredients showered down and around his plate.

Berke coughed politely in order to get his guest's attention. Other members of the family merely stared thunderstruck, eyes agog and jaws agape. Reb Avigdor's devoted disciples looked at one another uncomfortably; never before had they witnessed such outrageous behavior, and certainly not from their Rebbe!

Reb Avigdor was unfazed by the reactions. He continued to push, shove and stuff meat and potatoes, carrots and onions, and barley and lima beans into his gaping mouth as fast as he could scoop them up.

Berke's family and guests watched in dismay as their erstwhile meal disappeared before their eyes. Reb Avigdor was insatiable. What would make an ascetic who looked like he could survive on air suddenly eat like a boorish peasant? they wondered. Did he not know there were others at the table? Was he unaware of the scene he was causing?

When every globule of glutinous meat, every sliver of succulent potato, and every slice of sugar-sweet carrot were gone, Reb Avigdor asked innocently, "Do you have any more?"

Dumbfounded, Berke brought out the remainder. This, too, was devoured voraciously by his guest, down to the last scrap and morsel. When he finished he scraped the pot with the spoon one more time, as though to make sure that no vestige of what was once a colossal cholent remained around the rim.

"Is there any left?" Reb Avigdor asked when even the servants' portion was eaten up.

"Eh... no. I'm afraid not," a thoroughly shaken Berke lamented.

"Excellent. Really excellent," Reb Avigdor exclaimed. "That was a Shabbos meal to remember!"

"It certainly was!" Berke replied, still in a state of shock.

AFTER SHABBOS, it came time for the guests to bid their host good-bye. Reb Avigdor shook Berke's hand warmly, and related, "Our sages have declared that an act of hospitality is even greater than greeting the Divine Presence. We derive this lesson from the fact that God waited, as it were, while Avraham ran to invite the three angels disguised as men into his tent.

"My dear Berke, you too have fulfilled the mitzva in a manner worthy of Avraham Avinu."

"Thank you, Rabbi," Berke replied, still remembering his cholent. "And if you are ever in this area again, please stop by," he added somewhat unenthusiastically.

"It would be my pleasure," Reb Avigdor responded. "And please thank Masha for that wonderful cholent."

Once on the road, Reb Avigdor's *talmidim* respectfully kept quiet. They knew their Rebbe, and their Rebbe knew them.

After a long stretch of silence, he turned to them and defused the tension. "You know what my illustrious brother has said about living a life of holiness and avoiding luxury, how he has stressed that one's outer garb or appearance serves only as a reminder of the tenuousness of this world and the eternal promise of the World to Come." They all nodded pensively.

"So what then are your thoughts concerning my consuming the cholent?"

"You were trying to raise up certain holy sparks," answered one of his students.

"Not that I'm aware of," answered their master.

"You knew we were hungry, and wanted to prevent us from succumbing to our desires," said another.

"No, I didn't think of that either."

"You really wanted the mitzva of '*oneg*' on Shabbos?" proposed a third.

"Yes, but certainly not at everyone else's expense," Reb Avigdor responded.

"Maybe you were extremely hungry yourself?" suggested a fourth *talmid*, offering an ignoble explanation in his zeal to solve the mystery.

"You're right, I guess I was hungry... hungry to do a mitzva! As soon as I smelled the cholent, I knew something was wrong and my first taste confirmed my suspicion. Somehow Masha had flavored it with kerosene. If Berke had found out, I feared the poor girl would have been sent away on the spot. Something had to be done to save her position.

"But what about Berke?"

"I traded his ephemeral Shabbos meal in *Olam Hazeh* for something eternal."

"And what is that?" they all chimed in.

"The paramount mitzva of supporting an orphan — and meriting *Olam Habah*!"

The disciples, witnesses to Reb Yisrael of Ruzhin, admirers of Reb Chaim of Zanz, and adherents of Reb Avigdor Halberstam, exchanged a look of consummative understanding.

Heard from: Rabbi Chaim Twersky

As You Judge...

FOLLOWING *Maariv* a large crowd gathered around Rabbi Zvi Feldman, the yeshiva's *Mashgiach* and *Menahel*. His weekly talk, better known as a *shmuez*, concerning moral sensitivity and character perfection was always thought-provoking and inspirational. On this night, however, he outdid himself. Not only was the topic an important one, but everyone present realized how relevant and practical Rabbi Feldman's approach was.

As it happened, this was Rabbi Feldman's first talk in close to two months in which he didn't harp on what he felt was the students' biggest problem: the destruction of yeshiva property through recklessness and negligence.

"How," he usually demanded in each emotional talk, "can a student who spends hours of intense learning every day regarding torts — one ox goring another ox — not approach the yeshiva office and inquire how much he owes for damaging a chair, bending a fork, or cracking a cup?

"The hypocrisy is awesome," the Rabbi declared, "and one day you will have to account for it with a celestial bill that far exceeds dollars and cents."

It was no secret that the yeshiva was beset with a staggering budget crisis, a responsibility that fell squarely on Rabbi Feldman's shoulders. Clearly the last thing he needed was to cover prodigal expenses incurred by the yeshiva's own students. "We can't pay for heating and electricity," he was wont to repeat, "but we waste funds on repairing doors busted through negligence and heaters left on when no one is in the room."

Week after week the *Mashgiach* repeated similar accusations, for the situation had not improved. There was a bankruptcy with respect to *derech eretz kadma l'Torah*, and he felt that his students were sorely overdrawn.

Aside from his brilliant mind and gilt-edged character, the *Mashgiach* was also a skilled orator. He marshaled all of his oratorical abilities to strike at what he deemed to be the bane of yeshiva students' existence. Invariably his *shmuezim* were direct and devoid of bombast: pure, hard-core *mussar*, sometimes served with more than a dollop of sarcasm to prod the young students along.

IN A RECENT TALK leading up to the evening's *shmuez* Rabbi Feldman described a "typical" routine in the yeshiva. He began by poking fun at the lack of alacrity evinced when it came to rising for *Shacharis*, and continued: "... After four hours of intensive learning, including an hour of *shiur*, where your head is engaged in the most lofty and sublime pursuits, you must interrupt your study for *Mincha*. You gently plant a kiss on your *Gemara* and place it back on your *shtender* so that it will be ready after lunch.

"Preparations for *Mincha* include the proper attire, ablution, mental cogitations and emotional exertions, to ensure a meaningful spiritual rendezvous with the King of Kings. You are now ready. From the very commencement of the service you pour out your heart and *chop melachim*, ascending rung after rung of pietistic heights with your cherubic cohorts.

"But just as Yom Kippur must eventually come to an end by the consumption of a meal, you too must now replenish your bodily needs. Obviously eating is an unpleasant, mundane task that mandates exiting the hallowed study hall. But alas, you try and console yourself; thus has God fashioned man, and perforce there is no recourse.

"Resigned to your unpleasant lot, pining heartgrief and *cri du coeur* suddenly tear your heart asunder. There are only enough pieces of chicken on the tables to accommodate everyone present! Devouring a double portion will require activating a catalysis of enzymes and exercising an expeditious nimbleness not present earlier in the morning. Thus you leap into the dining room like a mad bull let loose at a matador. With herculean might you rip out the chair from under the table, splintering off a piece of formica in the sweep. In your rush to serve yourself the two largest pieces you mangle the fork, simultaneously thrusting a piece of bread into your mouth, a blessing for which you managed to utter faster than the speed of sound.

"Teeth engaged in a mauling operation even a hydraulically powered industrial grinder couldn't mimic, you pry the bones from between your lips with the realization that you can now relax. True, you may have appeared a bit barbaric on the outside, but on the holy inside the chicken has rejuvenated your spiritual innards. You take comfort in the knowledge that your intentions were wholly noble: you simply sought a speedy return to the study hall.

"But why do you consume that second piece of chicken so slowly, pray tell? Could it be, *chalila*, that you want to appear like the second group of *bochurim* arriving at the table to eat their singular piece of chicken? The fact that some boys sitting at your table will have to slink into the kitchen and explain to the cook that they did not have a portion is certainly of no concern to *you*. Where were these unfortunate shleppers during *mussar seder*, when the *Mesillas Yesharim* beckoned to one and all to learn the virtue of *zrizus*?

"In fact you are so relaxed you savor every bite of your second helping. For an extra measure of comfort you lean back, balancing yourself on the chair's back legs. However, this chair, like the rest of the yeshiva's venerable furniture, can no longer tolerate abuse, so the back of the chair wilts and creaks its way to a horrible demise. 'Dumb chair,' you mumble to yourself, as you thrust it to the side of the dining hall. It crashes into the wall with a loud thwack and a large flake of paint chips off, appropriately forming an ersatz *yahrzeit* plaque.

"DON'T YOU SEE what has happened?" the *Mashgiach* thundered, raising his voice. "In the one flight of stairs from the *beis midrash* to the dining hall you have descended from the angelic heights of the *talmid chacham* to the depths of a boorish animal!"

By this point everyone in the room was smiling, grinning, and even chuckling over the surrealistic picture Rabbi Feldman had painted. But then the *Mashgiach* changed his tone.

"Instead of laughing you should be grimacing! Even if some of you boys are plagued with acute schizophrenia, which renders you a *behaima* in yeshiva clothing — a pious fraud who sells the *zechuyos* of a year's *limud haTorah* and *mussar* study for a piece of greasy chicken — what right do you have to destroy and damage that which is not yours: yeshiva property purchased through precious *tzeddakah* funds!"

THE *MASHGIACH* pursued this conscience-raking topic for several weeks before opting for a new subject for the evening's *shmuez*: *dan l'kaf zechus* — judging favorably. The topic of the *shmuez* took the boys by surprise, for they knew that the *Mashgiach* and *Roshei Yeshiva* were still incensed over the numerous acts of reckless negligence still plaguing the deteriorating yeshiva.

Quoting the *Mishna* in *Pirke Avos*, "*hevei dan es kol ha'adam l'kaf zechus*," Rabbi Feldman began to expound upon the importance of this mitzva: "Notice that the *Mishna* employs the term *kol* **ha** *'adam*. This literally means 'the *whole* man,' not *every* man. The way to find merit in a fellow human being is to judge him as a whole. Every person has some redeeming qualities and altruistic motives — even if we cannot see every side of him from our perspective.

"But there is far more to judging favorably," continued the *Mashgiach*. The following *Gemara* (Shabbos 127b) was read to the *talmidim*:

> "He who judges his neighbor meritoriously will also be judged favorably. A story is told of a man who descended from the Upper Galilee to work in the south for three years. On *erev Yom Kippur*, at the end of his term of service, he requested from his employer,

'Give me my wages so that I may go and support my wife and children.'

"'I have no money,' answered the employer.

"'Then give me produce,' beseeched the worker.

"'I have none,' he replied.

"'Give me property.'

"'I have none.'

"'Give me livestock.'

"'I haven't any.'

"'Give me pillows and bedding.'

"'I have none.'

"The hired hand dejectedly slung his meager belongings over his shoulder and returned home.

"After the Sukkos festival the employer brought the wages to the worker's home, together with three laden asses, one bearing food, another drink, and the third various delicacies. They ate and the salary was paid.

"Afterwards the employer asked his worker: 'When you demanded, "Give me my wages," and I responded, "I have no money," of what did you suspect me?'

"'I thought that you might have spent my wages on a bargain that had just then presented itself.'

"'When I told you that I had no livestock what was in your thoughts?'

"'I thought that it may have been hired out to others.'

"'And when I said that I had no property?'

"'I thought that perhaps it had been leased to others.'

"'And when I told you that I did not have any produce, what did you believe was the truth?'

"'I thought that maybe it had not been tithed yet.'

"'What did you think when I told you that I had no pillows or bedding?'

"'I thought that maybe you had sanctified all of your property to the Temple.'

"'I swear to you!' he exclaimed, 'thus it was. Everything you thought was exactly how it happened!... And just as you have judged me favorably, so may God judge you the same way.'"

"This *Gemara*," commented the *Mashgiach*, "a story about a humble laborer named Akiva ben Yosef, who later became the famed Rabi Akiva, teaches us something that doubly challenges human nature. We are not only to judge favorably but to believe in the explanations we devise as well. What you may consider to be an absurd justification may actually be the truth!"

RABBI FELDMAN proceeded to relate incidents, some of them thoroughly amazing, to prove his point. The boys were visibly thrilled by his stories, nodding approvingly with every point. His novel but simple idea was slowly gaining acceptance: when you judge someone favorably, chances are that you are judging correctly.

The *shmuez* was followed by *Maariv*. Directly afterwards, as if rehearsed, the students surrounded the *Mashgiach* to discuss his thought-provoking *shmuez*. For an hour and a half they analyzed the dos and don'ts of *dan l'kaf zechus* with him. Rabbi Feldman was gratified by the way his talk was received. It was already late at night so he retired from the room, secure in the feeling that he had done his yeshiva and his students a service.

Before heading home, the Rabbi entered the yeshiva office to see if there were any messages recorded on the answering machine. Since he also served as the *Menahel*, his responsibilities extended beyond moral and spiritual matters. This straddling of two worlds was poignantly demonstrated by the removal of his full-brimmed fedora when he entered the administrative office.

RABBI FELDMAN walked into the sparse office and reflexively pushed down the button to activate the answering machine. But nothing happened. He verified that it was plugged in, but the recorder still didn't make a sound. The *Mashgiach* removed the lid and discovered, to his chagrin, that the special looped message tape was missing.

Rabbi Feldman searched the area in vain. How peculiar, he thought to himself. This tape, which he had purchased just three weeks earlier, was never removed from the machine since it was long enough to record dozens of messages. Rabbi Feldman's temples began to beat in frustration and anger.

"For six weeks," he found himself murmuring out loud, "I addressed the boys about not ruining or taking liberties with the property of the yeshiva, and this is the result!"

This act was far more audacious than any vandalism to date. A tape doesn't disappear from mere negligence. Until tonight the damage was confined to dorm rooms, the *beis midrash* and the dining room. But the *office* of all places!

What if the pledge of a large donation is lost forever on that missing tape? The *Mashgiach* considered keeping the premises locked and off limits to students from then on.

RABBI FELDMAN tried to figure out who could have perpetrated this outrage. He wished he could have attributed it to the yeshiva's secretary, the only other person who should ever touch the machine as part of her official duties. But that was an impossibility since she went home at five o'clock, and at 9:45 P.M., prior to the *shmuez,* he had turned on the answering machine. The missing tape was in its place a few short hours earlier.

Reviewing all of the relevant factors, the Rabbi distinctly remembered not locking the office door that evening. There was no need, he had reasoned, since everyone was inside the *beis midrash* for the *shmuez* and that was to be followed by *Maariv.*

His mind was actively at work trying to solve the puzzle and to ascertain the culprit. "Ironic," he thought to himself, "that just after a *shmuez* regarding '*dan l'kaf zechus*' such a meritless act had to occur. What positive motivation could ever be invented to justify the unauthorized removal of yeshiva property? Such an item would not be stolen and could not be borrowed. Someone out there wants to raise my blood pressure!"

In the midst of these ruminations, the *Mashgiach* was interrupted by the *Rosh Yeshiva*'s entrance into the office.

"YASHER KOACH, Reb Zvi," opened his colleague, "I never saw the boys get so animated from a *shmuez.* What did you talk about? Oh, and before you answer that, you have a few messages: Your brother-in-law from Monsey called and asked you to get back to him. Reb Naftali called regarding the Xerox machine and said that he thinks he has a buyer. Bernstein asked me to remind you that his *chupah* is beginning promptly. And Mrs. Neuman called... oh that was for her son. There, I'm sorry I interrupted myself. Now tell me, what was the *shmuez* about tonight?"

"The *shmuez* was about... a mistake," said the flustered *Mashgiach.* "For some reason I thought I could get off the subject of damaging yeshiva property, but I see I engaged in wishful thinking."

"What happened?" asked the *Rosh Yeshiva.*

"What happened is an act of brazen *chutzpah!* One of the boys — sometime between the *shmuez* and now — walked off with the tape to the answering machine... one second, did you just say that Neuman got a phone call?"

"Y... Yes."

"He was the only one not present at the *shmuez.* Although I just spoke about *dan l'kaf zechus* I find it very difficult to imagine what he was doing during that time."

No sooner had the *Mashgiach* finished saying these words when Neuman walked into the office with the cassette in his hand.

The eyes of the *Mashgiach* flared toward the boy in a fury of indignation. At last, he had caught the culprit red-handed!

A look of shame overcame the boy and he attempted to back out of the door. Rabbi Feldman arrested Neuman's escape and confronted him with an inquiring "Nu?"

Neuman began to toy nervously with one of the buttons on his jacket, at which point the *Rosh Yeshiva* excused himself and walked out of the office. Alone with the *Mashgiach*, the boy spoke in a soft, apologetic tone. "I'm sorry. Just before the *shmuez* my mother called on the office phone and we had a long, private conversation. After a little while, I heard a clicking noise, which made me realize that our conversation was inadvertently being taped. As soon as I hung up I took the tape to my room to erase it.

"I feel bad that I missed the *shmuez*, but my mother is beside herself regarding a family problem and I just couldn't tell her I'd call her back later.

"I was planning to find the *Mashgiach*," continued Neuman, lowering his voice, "as soon as I erased and returned the tape. You see, I may have to go home tomorrow morning. I know that it is very late, but if the *Mashgiach* would be so kind, I must discuss this matter..."

Neuman began to stutter, and tears poured forth from his eyes. "M... My father, I just found out this evening, has cancer..."

THE *MASHGIACH* placed a strong and sympathetic arm around the young student and sat him down in the office. He drew another chair closer for himself. "You weren't the only one," Rabbi Feldman said with visible emotion, both to the boy and to himself, "to miss the *shmuez* tonight." He wiped away a wistful tear, shut his eyes tightly, swayed back and forth with a low moan, and sought consolation for the both of them.

Heard from: Rabbi Dovid Hersh Mayer

All His ways are just

&

דע״י שלו דנתה למרע״ה לכף זכות לומר דמסתמא כדין עשה מה שפירש מאשתו חשבה הכתוב למדברת לשה״ר ממש ונענשה ע״ז בצרעת

חפץ חיים כלל ג במ״ח ס״ק: יא

Since Miriam did not judge Moshe Rabbeinu favorably and assume that his separation from his wife was in accord with the Law, the Torah reckoned her as one who had spoken Lashon Hara *and she was therefore punished with* tzara'as.

Chafetz Chaim Klall 3
Be'ar Mayim Chayim 11

Sustain Them in Famine

(Tehillim 33:19)

APRIL 14, 1945: Every day, and from every direction, the Allies were closing in on Nazi Germany. Inch by inch, they fought their way to its evil heart.

Three million combined Allied troops converged from the north and west. Another four million Russian soldiers were racing across from the east, while the British Second Army, led by Lieutenant-General Miles C. Dempsey, was spearheading the advance from the south.

The route of the Second Army was plotted on a course that would take it directly through the notorious concentration camp of Bergen-Belsen, a hideous, brutal symbol of man's most bestial inhumanity.

In the past month its population had swelled by 300 percent, and each new day brought a massive influx of thousands of victims. Men, women, and especially children arrived with the Germans retreating from the east. Driven for hundreds of miles in forced marches which lasted for weeks, the pathetic, disoriented new prisoners were starved and disease-ridden.

Not surprisingly, the death rate was horrifying: in the month of March alone, more than twenty thousand Jews had perished at the camp. Not content to let nature take its course, the Nazis placed Bergen-Belsen under the direction of an expert — the notorious mass-murderer and former commandant of Auschwitz, Josef Kramer.

The new commander immediately contrived to turn the camp into even more of a veritable hell, if that was possible, for the miserable inmates. The dead in Bergen-Belsen quickly exceeded the crematoria's capacity to dispose of them. It simply could not "process" the bodies quickly enough, so the innumerable corpses were heaved on top of each other around the barracks and burned in the open.

The major task of the Nazis was no longer just to kill as many Jews as they could. Now that the Fatherland itself was being overrun, they were making feverish attempts to cover their tracks and eliminate signs of their terrible atrocities. For the *coup de grâce*, Hitler had ordered that all concentration camps, including Bergen-Belsen, be destroyed by bombing prior to the arrival of the Allied forces. At least this would ensure the "final solution" and ultimate destruction of all the Jewish souls contained within the camps.

HIMMLER, however, the head of the infamous, merciless Gestapo, had no trouble predicting the future. He tried desperately to salvage something from the abysmal inferno into which Germany had finally descended, and attempted to negotiate peace with Britain and the United States. Simultaneously, leaders of influential Jewish organizations outside Nazi-occupied Europe were exploiting every possible means of exerting influence on the Nazi chieftain.

One such leader was Hillel Storch, a representative of the World Jewish Congress in Sweden. In a meeting with Felix Kersten, Himmler's personal physician, Storch diplomatically pointed out that it would be in Himmler's best interests to countermand Hitler's latest directive. The advancing Allied forces, he argued, might view with favor Himmler's intervention to prevent the bombing and obliteration of all the concentration camps.

Storch's valiant efforts were succcessful. As Germany's military collapse became even-more inevitable, Himmler displayed a willingness — even an eagerness — to prove his magnanimity toward the pathetic remnant of European Jewry still languishing in the death camps. He agreed to ignore Hitler's order for the final annihilation.

A new command was issued: all concentration camp survivors were to be relinquished to the approaching armies. On April 3, 1945, rumors of the increasingly appalling conditions prompted Storch to express specific concern regarding the fate of Bergen-Belsen's inmates. Kersten responded with an assurance from Himmler himself that Bergen-Belsen would be surrendered to the British military in an orderly fashion.

Meanwhile, news of the sweeping Allied advance spread rapidly through the camp; small groups of prisoners huddled secretly to hear and pass on the latest information. They were no longer hoping against hope, slowly counting the months, the years, to liberation and wondering whether they could possibly survive. Their freedom was imminent. Indeed, if they listened carefully, they could hear the faint, distant sounds of battle, sounds that grew louder — and closer — with each passing day.

BEFORE LONG, there were signs within the camp that the end was finally approaching. For the inmates of "Stern Camp," the smallest of the subdivisions within Bergen-Belsen, the writing appeared on the wall when it was announced that bread rolls would be served to them. "We want you to tell the British how *nicely* we treated you," the German guards said insidiously.

Pandemonium broke out. The mere thought of bread rolls caused the starving, emaciated prisoners to erupt in an outpouring of rapturous joy. During these last weeks, a minute quantity of muddy water, disguised as coffee, had been a luxury that was occasionally served to a privileged few. But for the overwhelming majority of detainees, going without food or drink for days at a stretch had been the norm.

Parched, dry mouths began to salivate. Inmates who had feared they would never eat again formed long, interminably slow-moving lines outside the barracks where the Nazis grudgingly distributed a small, white, fresh roll to spellbound recipients.

ALEXANDER WEISZ, possessed of a thin, wizened face, shaven head and skeletal frame, was among the pathetic wretches who stood in line. He had already endured the inhuman deprivations of two other death camps and had suffered every horror imaginable; he had witnessed every nightmare let loose upon the earth by the Nazi demons.

Still, waiting outside the barracks he stopped wondering for a moment about the fate of other members of his family, whether any of them had survived the Nazi regime. He was now obsessed by a single, macabre thought: that his turn would never come.

Every last ounce of his energy and willpower was intently focusing upon the act of survival, on merely withstanding the endless, seemingly motionless bread line. At this minute, given the choice between liberation and a fistful of a soft, doughy roll, every one of the famished, gasping prisoners pushing and shoving in the April cold, including Alexander, would have unquestioningly grabbed the roll.

As each inmate stepped forward to the head of the line, the precious bun would be clutched tightly and the prisoner would move off in a daze. The anticipation and frenzied excitement were palpable. Only in the demonic hell of Bergen-Belsen, or any of its counterparts in the Holocaust kingdom of death, could the prospect of a small roll cause such euphoria and unbounded pleasure.

Every foot, every inch, toward the front of the line was compulsively measured: How much farther? How much longer before the bread basket would come into view? How soon could their eyes, at least, could feast on the miraculous paradox of murderous Nazi fingers placing life-saving food into innocent Jewish hands?

ALEXANDER counted only forty people ahead of him and his adrenaline surged. As he craned his neck and strained his eyes, a wondrous sight emerged: bread being dispensed from a huge basket. As he drew closer he could almost see inside the bread basket. He stood up on his toes, and was seized by fright: the basket was almost empty.

A searing combination of fear and panic threatened to overcome him. His heart pounded thunderously, about to explode out of his scrawny chest. Never, through all of the horrors he had experienced, had he felt so stricken with sheer terror. Having been promised a piece of bread after so much deprivation, Alexander could no longer endure another day of starvation. He dreaded his hunger more than he did an SS officer brandishing a truncheon. Drained and exhausted by his day-long wait in line he mustered his last reserves of strength to measure the rolls left in the basket against the number of prisoners ahead of him.

One more step forward; it was his turn. Wide-eyed, he watched in utter relief as the Nazi withdrew the very last roll and thrust it into his outstretched, cupped hands. Alexander's fingers closed tightly around it.

Before he stepped out of line, he caught sight of a plentiful supply of rolls. Tremendous piles were stacked up at the end of the barracks and he saw one of the guards remove a fresh basket.

Suddenly, an idea sent Alexander's mind racing. His highly developed instinct for survival activated every starving cell in his brain. He knew that to the Nazis, all Jews — like cows, or pigs — looked alike. Indeed, in his grim experience they barely ever looked at Jews as human beings. Thus, if he hid the roll and simply remained in line, he would receive another one.

Two rolls — double rations! So enticing was the thought, so beguiling the image, that Alexander could hardly tear himself away from the plan and concentrate on the possibility of being caught. There was, he knew only too well, but one possible consequence: instant death.

He debated and deliberated: Would just one roll be enough to sustain him until the camp's liberators arrived? He had no idea; he certainly had no guarantee. As he weighed the risks, his emotions did not enable him to think rationally. He simply could not resolve his dilemma... until circumstance solved it for him. Unexpectedly, as though an apparition had materialized from thin air, the Nazi was standing in front of him again, laden with bread rolls. Petrified, Alexander froze on the spot.

"Next," roared the German impatiently.

Without knowing how he summoned the courage, Alexander uttered a grunt indicating his turn. The German jabbed a roll at him, and he was summarily shoved out of line. Relieved of the awful ordeal at last, Alexander resumed breathing.

BUT HIS RELIEF was premature. A large, fleshy hand clamped his shoulder in a vise-like grip and spun him round. In anticipation of the downward stroke of a club on his skull, Alexander cowered involuntarily, covering his head with his arms. He waited for the blow, but nothing happened. Slowly, he opened his eyes, turned his head upwards, and found a brawny Russian prisoner looming above him.

"Jew," he snarled, "I saw that! Give me that extra roll."

For Alexander, time stood still: he could hardly comprehend that he was being confronted not by a Nazi guard but by a fellow prisoner, who was aggressively demanding that which did not belong to him. Relieved, he quickly regained his composure.

"Nothing doing!" he countered firmly. "I risked my life for this roll. I am not about to give it to you!"

A simple snap of the fingers from the Russian brought his comrades — the only other non-Jews in the camp — to his side. The Russians seized the moment. In a flash they overcame Alexander, snatching both of the rolls from him. The Jewish inmates who witnessed the incident were not about to imperil what was left of their own pathetic lives over a minor "injustice." Besides, the Russian hadn't yet settled the score.

The brute looked down at the young Jew who now lay at his feet and a menacing grin slowly spread across his face. Then the beating began. He kicked Alexander twice in the face, mauled his jaw with his elbow, and kicked the helpless Jew in the groin, sending him writhing in pain across the barracks floor. The Russian had often observed the SS guards mete out such punishment, and obviously he enjoyed mimicking their ways.

For the first time in three-and-a-half years of suffering, agony and unadulterated torture, tears welled up in Alexander's eyes. Before long, he was weeping uncontrollably. They were the first tears he had shed since the Nazi darkness had descended.

He had survived because he was strong and had not allowed the nightmare to break his soul. But now, crawling in agony on the barracks floor, blood oozing from his forehead and mouth, shaking from wounds inflicted by a fellow prisoner, he had no defenses left.

Swarms of insects descended upon the cadaverous figure sprawled on the squalid, dirt-encrusted floor, their buzzing echoing maddeningly in his ears. Undoubtedly, the vermin and lice must have taken him for dead, and they feasted unintermittently on his emaciated body.

For Alexander, the world had become a crucible of exquisite, unremitting pain. The tears scorched his face, like burning rivulets coursing down his cheeks and into cuts and open sores. But it all paled in comparison with the pain of the emptiness in his stomach. In over three years of existence on the brink of starvation, he had never been as hungry as he was now. He was hungry enough to die.

ANGER BURNED inside him. The Allied troops were practically at the camp gates and, after all his travail, they would find him, like so many others, a hideous corpse discarded outside the barracks.

"Why, why, WHY!" he demanded. "Why did God have to abandon me now? There were so many other times I could have died and been spared from enduring any more of this torture. Why now, when freedom is just a few hours away..."

Alexander wondered if his hunger and broken spirit would let him fall asleep and put him out of his misery. Waiting for the end to come, he lay there crying to God from the depths of his soul, searching for a meaning to it all, desperately trying to articulate his bitterness. "You have betrayed me in my final hour," he sobbed. "You have deserted me without cause. Now, at least let me die, and be done with it all!"

THE NEXT MORNING, Alexander awoke. At first he could not tell whether he was alive or dead. He was aware that his eyes were blinking in the morning light, that his body ached with pain, but something just wasn't right.

"The Nazis," he realized suddenly; "where are the Nazis?" Inspection was always conducted before dawn, when the barracks reverberated with harsh, nasal curses and cracks of the whip.

Bewildered by the strangest sensations he had ever felt, he raised himself off the floor with difficulty. Seeing the sun blazing high in the sky he was now no longer sure if he was still alive.

Looking around, he shivered with horror. He was not

alone. The other inmates were also in the barracks, crammed in as tightly as ever. But nobody stirred; they... they were all dead.

Alexander was standing in the middle of a charnel house, and he was the only one left alive. All at once he understood what had happened: the bread of liberation, the rolls the Nazis had generously handed out to them the day before, had all been poisoned.

Heard from: Rabbi Yitzchak Chinn

A Toast to Life

THE BATTLE OF YPRES was finally over. Although victory had been won at a catastrophic cost heretofore unknown in terms of loss of life and property, World War I continued, a seemingly ceaseless nightmare of slaughter and horror.

Even the imperturbable German Field Marshal, a man who reveled in war's glories, could no longer shrug off its terrible toll. He willed that it would all be over soon. At sixty-three, he had reached life's contemplative phase, something only too apparent now on his worried, preoccupied countenance.

He no longer looked as young as he would have liked, nor as debonair. His body was heavy on its frame and his muscles sagged more from inactivity and desk work than from overindulgence and gluttony. His eyebrows — wild, bushy, white wings — were slanted into a ferocious "V," and his nose was red and puffy, covered with massive constellations of blue-red blood vessels. Even his usually bright eyes were faded.

The Field Marshal's brilliant attacks at Neuve Chapelle, Aubers Ridge, Festubert and Givency seemed like ancient history. Glorious victories were now meaningless, useless memories ever since the flower of his army had been massacred on Hill 69.

The mutilated, ravaged bodies of dead German soldiers bore silent testimony to ignominious, shattering defeat. Stunned eyewitnesses told haltingly of the deluge of bombs, which rained down upon the struggling masses of men, and of their desperate and frantic attempts to escape the fate of the countless thousands sprawled outside the tilted beams of dugouts and shelters, a ghastly corroboration of the lethality of chemical warfare. Traumatized survivors vividly described scenes of shattered skulls and disfigured faces, missing hands, legs, arms, feet — horrifying heaps of limbs everywhere. Both the communication and assembly trenches were choked to overflowing with dead soldiers piled one upon the other, three or four deep.

Morale was low. Almost overcome by the disaster, the Field Marshal prayed desperately for good tidings. Along with the incredible loss of troops, some of his most cherished officers had perished on Hill 69 and he was impatient to take revenge on the British.

SMALL WONDER that news of a victory swept rapidly throughout the German ranks, arresting the stifling depression of defeat and bringing a glimmer of cheer to the haggard, hang-dog faces of the soldiers. Oberleutnant Heinz Müller, commanding just three German regiments, with one Jager battalion in support, had managed to outwit the British and breach their lines at two points at the front. With machine guns blazing at short range while long-range guns fired gas shells, the 47th London and the 15th Scottish divisions defending Hill 70 had been caught off guard by the German enfilade. Thus, the vitally strategic site had been recaptured.

Bursting with pride, and basking in the glory of German military prowess, the Field Marshal left his headquarters at St. Omer to personally inspect the aftermath of Müller's miracle. From the distant slopes of Hill 70, twelve kilometers away on the right, to the Hulluch-Vermelles road on his left, all was now securely under German control. The Lens-La Bassee road was well protected by seven-meter-deep rolls of barbed-wire hedge as thick as brambles, and the narrow roads to Noeux-les-Mines and Bethune were patrolled by units equipped with gas canisters. Most of the enemy's trenches were blown in, their retaining structures blown out — what remained was just a hint of their previous existence.

The Field Marshal surveyed the scene of the battle with deep satisfaction. His eyes, shot with a tracery of blood, were unusually moist as he gazed upon the loamy soil of Hill 70, pocked and gashed with craters and destroyed trenches. Scattered all about were the chalk-white, kiltless bodies of the bulleted dead. Some had obviously been gassed, and others had been devastated by gunfire and mighty explosives, leaving a hideous collage of severed limbs and fractured bones protruding from bloodied uniforms and muddy boots.

The Field Marshal was ebullient and warmly embraced the young lieutenant who had masterminded and led the attack. "Your success in this battle will not go unrewarded," he assured Müller, pointing to the insignia on his epaulette. Then, slapping him heartily on the back, he returned to his staff car.

CHATEAU PHILOMEL, the regional headquarters six kilometers south of Lillers, was the next stop on the itinerary of the Field Marshal and his entourage. The high-ranking officers billeted there had just learned that the Field Marshal was touring their area, and they hastily prepared to greet him. His visits were always festive occasions, and scouts were dispatched to the closest checkpoints to announce his arrival. But before the scouts could get very far, sentries alerted the regional commander concerning the approach of their most distinguished guest.

By the time the shiny black Mercedes had clambered up to the front gate, everyone stationed at the chateau had lined up outside. The regional commander shouted "Achtung!" and the corps of officers snapped into a straight line. Upright, with their chins drawn in and the backs of their powerful necks bulging outward, they maintained their rigid posture throughout the Field Marshal's inspection of the guard.

The Field Marshal was the archetypical example for them all to follow: the silver spindle atop his jet-black helmet glinted in the morning sun and his neatly pressed uniform was decorated with a twisted, green shoulder cord — everything about his impeccable appearance indicated that he was the definitive model of the German soldier. He clicked his heels and bowed stiffly, effectively dismissing the men.

"GENTLEMEN," he announced proudly to those who gathered later in the lounge of the chateau, "thanks to Oberleutnant Müller's brilliant strategy, Foch, who commands the 10th French Army, is on the run."

A spontaneous, robust cheer of "Hurrah!" greeted the

news. The officers had all suffered from the French and welcomed the good tidings, but some regretted that Müller was the cause of them. On the outside there was a look of victorious unity: The officers' moustaches were brushed and waxed, with the ends twirled toward their ear lobes, and the peaks of their caps were perfectly aligned above their eyebrows.

Unobtrusively, however, some officers broke ranks. They were not happy that Müller, a Jew, was being honored as an army hero. They conspired to discredit and dishonor him. But it would not be easy considering the Field Marshal's infatuation with Müller and his military accomplishments.

It was a catastrophic coincidence, as Müller was to discover later, that while these jealous murmurings against him were circulating among the officers at the chateau, the Field Marshal would choose that precise moment to publicly honor him. Even as the Oberleutnant was beckoned to his patron's side, the detractors were plotting assiduously to find some pretext to disgrace him. Müller feared that his downfall was inevitable.

Oblivious to the scheming subterfuge and conspiratorial undercurrents swirling around his protégé, the Field Marshal announced: "Let us propose a toast to Oberleutnant Müller."

"*Jawohl*," responded the dry-throated officers, eager to comply. Most of the men moved towards the regional commander in order to fill their glasses with champagne. But a blanched Heinz Müller, strangely enough, stared into his already full glass with horror.

Müller was a dedicated soldier and, paradoxically, a devoted Jew. He had neither grown up in an observant home nor pursued formal Jewish studies, yet he adhered faithfully to whatever his upstairs neighbor — the beloved Rabbi of his hometown of Weiden — had taught him. His commitment to Judaism actually consisted of no more than a simple daily prayer, the setting aside of a tenth of his wages for charity, and one other seemingly simple promise.

The Rabbi of Weiden was an astute man. He abhorred the thought of Müller volunteering for the army, but he realized that he could not prevent him. There was very little in the realm of mitzvos that he could request a soldier stationed at the front to do. To expect Heinz to keep kosher or to observe Shabbos was futile, but there was, he believed, one thing he could demand, which could serve as a reminder that Müller was a Jew in a non-Jewish environment: not to drink gentile wine.

The Rabbi understood that honoring this prohibition might present, on occasion, an inconvenience or cause for embarrassment. Nonetheless, he maintained, it was feasible, and would maintain the fine line of separation between Heinz and his gentile comrades, which could be strengthened after military discharge. Furthermore, he promised the young conscript that the hardships he might undergo in keeping this precept would protect him.

Müller had taken a vow of abstinence from wine, and was now horrified by his promise. At this moment of supreme honor, spasms of nausea tore at his body. What was he to do? Obviously, he could not decline the drink on religious grounds, for he was keenly aware of the animosity that was already fermenting against him because he was Jewish. But to violate his word was equally unthinkable.

AS THE GLASSES were being handed out, the building vibrated from the din of airplanes overhead. It was odd for fighter planes to be flying over the area at that particular time of day, and some of the officers quipped that zeppelins should be ordered to fly missions whenever beverages were being served. Meanwhile, Müller thought of an idea.

He rushed to the window, pretending to look up at the aircraft. Actually he was alarmed by what he saw, for the planes looked far more like a French reconnaissance patrol than a Luftwaffe squadron. The matter at hand, however, quickly made him forget his military concerns. He waited until the drinks had been poured before turning toward the room, and then remained adjacent to the window.

A toast was declared: "*Zum Wohl Oberleutnant Müller*!" The officers raised their glasses and drank down their champagne. When Heinz was sure that everyone was savoring his drink, he spilled the contents of his glass out the window behind him.

He then moved nimbly back to his position next to the Field Marshal, to thank him for the honor. Embraces were exchanged and the Field Marshal prepared to depart. He waved regally to the gathering before his final salute, which signaled the end of the party.

LATER THAT AFTERNOON, as Müller sat enjoying the quiet and the beauty of the chateau's gardens, he marveled at his good fortune: The Field Marshal had showered the highest praises on him in front of his fellow officers, and had promised him a promotion. He had even managed to keep his pledge to the Rabbi. But his self-congratulations were premature...

Heinz Müller was suddenly confronted by three hostile superior officers, men whose vitriolic anti-Semitism knew no bounds. Their displeasure over the festivities of the day was glaring.

"*Herr* Müller," snarled a Colonel contemptuously, "we saw you throw your champagne out the window this morning."

Frozen with dread, Heinz had no response.

"What's the matter, Jew?" demanded the second officer. "Struck dumb?"

"The Kaiser's wine isn't good enough for you Jews?" hissed the third.

The Colonel grabbed a fistful of Müller's shirtfront, spat in his face and shook him so hard that his head spun on his neck. For the *coup de grâce*, he thrust him violently backwards, throwing him to the ground.

"I always thought," sneered the Colonel, "that a serious error in judgement was made in allowing a Jew, especially an ungrateful one such as you, to mix with his social superiors at Chateau Philomel. We have therefore arranged for your immediate transfer to the eastern front, a place where scum like you belong. The advancing Russians will no doubt benefit from your 'brilliant' military tactics," he concluded superciliously.

Müller lay where he had fallen, afraid to move. Blood was oozing out of the back of his head and down his neck, and he realized that his very survival depended on not provoking these men any further. He cowered, fighting the urge to weep. His military achievement would mean nothing on a front where conditions were deplorable and "past glories" were something only read about in history books. The Russian counteroffensive was steadily gaining momentum, pushing back the German lines. Müller knew that a trip to the front could very well be a one-way journey.

But more than any emotion coursing through Müller's head at that very moment was the fury he felt toward his Rabbi. Not only had his "holy law" gotten him into so much trouble, but the Rabbi had repeatedly assured him that observance of this mitzva would protect him. Some protection this had proven to be! Utterly humiliated, Müller cursed the Rabbi in disgust.

WELL BEFORE DAWN the following morning, Müller was placed on a train headed for the eastern front. The Colonel had insured that the decision would be implemented immediately, before someone close to the Field Marshal heard about it and had a chance to intercede. But it was unlikely, Müller reasoned, that even the Field Marshal would come to his defense after hearing of the contempt he had demonstrated for the toast in his honor.

Overcome by his bitter thoughts, he appeared to be in a trance when the train arrived at its first stop along the long route. A major was waiting at the depot to apprise the officers aboard of the tragedy that had occurred just after sunrise that morning. A squadron of French bombers had descended upon Chateau Philomel and the surrounding area, leveling every building and killing or wounding every single inhabitant. The site had been located on a reconnaissance run the previous day.

Heinz Müller was thunderstruck. "A protection," the Rabbi had said. He silently thanked the Rabbi, and prayed he would return to Weiden in health in order to learn the rest of God's commandments from his very special upstairs neighbor.

Heard from: Rabbi Yosef Fabian

In Your Blood, Live!
(Yechezkel 16:6)

THE 150,000-STRONG Jewish community of Lvov, Poland, was just one of the casualties of the German-Soviet war. The local Ukrainians welcomed the invading German forces and joined them in brutally pouncing upon the Jews. Jewish property was confiscated or looted, while synagogues and cemeteries were desecrated or destroyed. The Jewish community was fined twenty million rubles (four million dollars) for damage it had not caused, shunted into a ghetto, and forced to wear yellow badges — a mere prelude and mild beginning to *Aktion* upon monstrous *Aktion*. Tens of thousands were killed outright and the remainder were carted off to death camps, particularly Belzec and the Janowska Road Camp in Lvov.

One fateful night a major *Aktion* was launched to render Lvov thoroughly *Judenrein*. Electric arc lights were illuminated, and a large SS detachment together with three times as many local militias broke into squads of four to six men and swiftly entered the houses. When the inhabitants did not respond to the banging, the locked doors and windows were forced open with crowbars or blown apart with hand grenades.

The frightened residents were driven into the street just as they were, regardless of whether they were properly dressed or just in night clothes. With the aid of gunshots, ferocious dogs, whips, kicks and blows with rifle butts, the Jews were forced out of their homes in such haste that small children were often left behind in bed. Women in the streets cried for their children, and children wailed for their parents.

The hounded and wounded were beaten as they ran to a waiting freight train. Car after car was filled, and horrible scenes were witnessed: young mothers were roughly torn away from the infants they held; brothers and sisters clinging to one another were separated; little children ran about, devastated and crying in anguish; and youngsters pulled and dragged their dead parents to the train by their arms and legs.

The orders "Open the door! Open the door!" accompanied by cracking whips, barking dogs, rifle shots, desperate gasps and shrieks and wails echoed throughout the night.

JANOWSKA was initially established as a forced-labor camp for Lvov's Jews, but its officers derived so much enjoyment from the torture and murder of the inmates that it was converted into an extermination camp not only for the local Jews, but for tens of thousands of Jews who were transported from eastern Galicia.

Life in the camp was an unbelievable nightmare. At five

o'clock in the morning the doors of the barracks were unlocked, and exhausted, emaciated figures moved as briskly as they could through the latrines. Just weeks before these ghosts had been well-dressed, healthy individuals. Now their feet were wrapped in straw and their clothes were ragged. The conditions, on top of excruciatingly cold weather, had driven all human expression from their faces.

Terrible disorder prevailed in the latrines. The prisoners crowded around wildly, sullying each other. The overseers attempted to maintain a semblance of order, and if they caught someone dirtying the wall or floor, they were furious and turned him over to a slimy old man known as "Herr Doktor."

From the latrines the Jews were soon driven out into the inspection yard, where Herr Obersturmführer Gebauer, the camp commandant, and his deputy, Untersturmführer Wilhaus, were waiting. A gruesome charade known as "formation procedure" began with the Untersturmführer's command: "*Achtung*! Caps off!" followed by "Caps on! Number off!" This order required each inmate in line to recite a number in sequence. A slip of the tongue by any of the ill and intimidated wretches could be fatal. Likewise, one who didn't number off quickly enough when his turn came was set upon by two Scharführers and beaten unconscious with rubber truncheons and whips. Then the numbering off started over again until an inadvertent slipup brought about another beating. This was repeated at least twenty times. Then the prisoners went through a "Caps on! Caps off!" exercise thirty times. In this case, too, the Scharführers were no less diligent in teaching the virtue of German order and precision.

The Askaris, Russian prisoners of war employed in the camp, were instructed to beat the Jews with all their might, and they eagerly complied. In fact, they wielded their spiked bludgeons with such clockwork regularity that it appeared to be purely a reflex action on their part, if not a way of keeping warm.

AFTER FORMATION the day was devoted to sadistic entertainment for the bloodthirsty masters. One work brigade was ordered to collect car parts that had become frozen into the ground. The prisoners had to labor without gloves, and suffered relentless blows from the SS men and Askaris for their slow progress.

A different column of men was ordered to bear a dismantled truck body on its collective shoulders and parade around in a circle, without semblance of purpose, for hours on end. The perpetual blows to these men's heads could be heard from far away.

The sole object of work at Janowska was to provide the captors with the pleasure of torturing their captives. The delight they derived from inflicting suffering was boundless. Their favorite method was to impose fictitious meaning on meaningless work. Thus, the daily march had to be orderly; yet it was organized so as to produce inevitable chaos. This was not irreconcilable in view of the Nazi "logic of destruction" perfected at Janowska.

Jews had to be clean-shaven, but it was strictly forbidden to possess a razor or scissors. No button could be missing from the striped inmate suit, but if you lost one at work, which was unavoidable, there was no way to replace it. The prisoners had to be strong, but were systematically weakened. Once you entered the camp, everything was confiscated, but you were then spat on by robbers because you owned nothing.

According to concentration camp law, a louse

discovered during a shirt check meant capital punishment not just because it could infest its host with typhus, which meant certain death, but because any prisoner on whom a louse was observed after a delousing order had been issued had obviously failed or refused to obey orders and therefore had to be severely disciplined. That water was not available or that the inmates had neither soap nor a towel was irrelevant.

On the one hand, the prisoners had to "keep clean," and therefore had to relieve themselves at places set aside for this purpose. But on the other hand, they could not just wander off from work or roll call to do so.

They were forbidden to go to the latrines, but they were also suffering from increasingly severe dysentery, caused and aggravated by rancid soup as well as constant cold. Naturally they would try, but when their absences were noticed they would be subject to harsh punishment.

JANOWSKA'S OBERSTURMFUHRER personally oversaw the torture, and made periodic rounds to see that things were going "just right." One day he saw an old man who was obviously straining every nerve and sinew in an effort to keep pace with the other workers, but he could not. Menacingly, the Obersturmführer asked why he was working so slowly. The man replied that he didn't have the energy to work any faster. The commandant then drew his revolver, dangled it as he always did to terrorize the victim as much as possible, and then summarily shot the poor man in the head. As if he had merely crushed a beetle underfoot, the officer resumed his inspection unmoved.

One treacherously cold January day, the Obersturmführer ordered seven healthy, robust young

Jews to strip and climb into a freshly filled vat of water, proclaiming, "You swine won't wash yourselves otherwise." After two hours, frigid chunks of ice could be broken off the corpses.

A Jewish street singer whose pleasant melodies everyone loved stood on the edge of a pit, mixing lime. Convinced that he was working too slowly, the Obersturmführer pushed him in, where he slowly and agonizingly burned to death in the corrosive cauldron.

Members of the "compulsion brigade" were forced to pick up huge stones far too heavy for an ordinary man to lift. Their inability to raise such stones was considered sufficient reason for inhuman punishment.

When the Ober- and Untersturmführer wished to practice "sharpshooting," they stood at the window of their office and used the prisoners who happened to pass by as moving targets. They aimed for the hand, the nape of the neck, the knee, or the nose. Once they finished their practice, they went about the camp, seeking out those who had been wounded — even if only if the finger — and gave them a "mercy shot" in the head.

IN THE EVENING, "dinner" was served — a repulsive, malodorous broth made of rotten turnips. This was followed by two hours of brutality in the inspection yard, after which the prisoners would be locked in for the night in their overcrowded barracks — lacking sanitary facilities, and teeming with carnivorous bugs and lice.

On a periodic basis, there were sudden uproars at night and the door to their jail was thrown open. Askaris so drunk they could barely stand upright would reel in and proceed to run amok, striking out left and right with their clubs. They would engage in this amusement for the better part of two hours, leaving every inmate bleeding and wounded. Only then would they clear out and lock the door behind them.

The Nazi logic of destruction was aimed, ultimately, at the victim's suicide. Each and every atrocity was premeditated for this purpose. By forbidding a prisoner to use a toilet, own anything, or become in any way slovenly, even though this was impossible, an overwhelming self-disgust would develop in the victim, to the point that he would desire death. This self-destruction was to be preceded by a self-transformation into the loathsome creature that, according to Nazi doctrine, the Jew had been since birth. Thus, degradation, humiliation, cruelty and torture were all means to achieve this fundamental goal.

"GIVE ME A KNIFE!" demanded the pale young woman. Only a couple of the inmates even bothered to look at her.

"A knife?" mused a middle-aged Jew slaving at a meaningless activity. "That's a novel approach." Since their arrival at Janowska many of the prisoners had secretly sought poison as a way to end their miserable existence. But this was the first announcement of a desire that Jews — to the great chagrin of the Germans — never expressed openly.

Her request alerted an SS guard, who quickly removed his truncheon to silence the disturbance. He turned to the frail woman and sneered, "What do you want, you cursed dog?"

The woman neither trembled nor cowered, which made the officer uncomfortable. He raised his truncheon to unleash a blow that would surely have put an end to her unbidden courage.

But the woman looked straight up at the guard and met his eyes. Without a trace of panic she related calmly, "I want a knife."

The German lowered his arm and revealed a gruesome leer. Still brandishing the truncheon, he rested his hands on his belt and began to chortle. His victim, in the meantime, had locked her feverish eyes on the upper pocket of his uniform, where the outline of a knife was clearly discernible.

"Give me that knife!" the woman repeated, pointing her finger at the same time. The German dropped his smile and, remarkably, obeyed. A hush fell upon all the witnesses, and although they realized that they were risking their lives by stopping their work — even for a second — they remained transfixed by this suicidal madwoman.

"She couldn't wait until nightfall," an angry Jew standing on the side whispered to his comrade, "and let the Askaris do the job. Since when do we have to give them the satisfaction in public?" Other Jews around him agreed, and they regarded this crazy woman with disgust.

The woman circumspectly took the knife and placed it in her right hand before bending down to a bundle of rags at her feet. Deliberately yet tenderly, she unraveled the rags, revealing a newborn baby sleeping on a white pillow. The mother raised her baby, drew the knife close and pronounced in an intense, unfrightened voice: "Blessed are You, Lord our God, King of the Universe, who has sanctified us through Your commandments, and instructed us to perform the circumcision."

Meticulously, she performed the sacred rite, as tears

streamed down her wan and bony cheeks. Standing upright and proud, she turned heavenward and proclaimed in a voice muffled with emotion: "Master of the Universe, You were kind enough to deliver to me a healthy child and I have done what I can to insure a perfect, kosher Jew."

Affectionately hugging her whimpering baby, she walked back to the awed soldier and returned his bloodstained knife.

Heard from: Pia Weinstein

The judge knot

❦

והוא דן אותו לכ״ח ובשביל זה הלך וגינהו לבד שעבר בזה על בצדק תשפוט עמיתך עוד עבר בזה על איסור סיפור לשון הרע.

חפץ חיים כלל ג:ז

And if one judges and deprecates his fellow man where he is halachically forbidden to do so, not only has he transgressed the commandment of "Judge your People justly," he has violated the interdiction of Lashon Hara.

Chafetz Chaim Klall 3:7

Give Me Shelter

HE CALLED HIMSELF Pincus, but he was better known as "the Professor." And just as he had no name, he had no home. Instead, he wandered from place to place, and from town to town, staying where he could for as long as he could. If you asked him where he was last, he would sigh and tell you that due to man's inhumanity to man, he had been forced to sleep in a variety of locales over the past several weeks, ranging from a bus station in New York to a park bench in Philadelphia.

Pincus ate sporadically and sparingly, his fare usually consisting of whatever his co-religionists could provide. Although he never asked for anything special, he did have a penchant for eggs, which was advantageous because he had been served thousands of them during the weeks and months and years that he had been on the road.

Actually, no one really knew how long he had been wandering. It seemed that he had been doing it forever, almost like the hidden mystics of old who would spend their time in a self-imposed exile, doing mitzvos and helping others. And maybe, just maybe, he was one of them: a man who spent his life giving others the opportunity to fulfill the mitzva of *hachnasas orchim*.

Admittedly, not everyone subscribed to this theory. The local rabbi and the caretaker of the Hebrew Sheltering Society of Scranton, Pennsylvania, certainly did not. To them the Professor was just another drifting soul who came often and stayed longer than most at their facility.

OVER THE YEARS, Rabbi Daniel Gellman had seen and served hundreds of Jews, who for one reason or another ended up on the steps of the Hebrew Sheltering Society. There was the young Israeli who had met an American girl in Haifa and followed her halfway around the world, only to find out that she couldn't even remember his name. And the father of a seven-year-old girl from Montreal, who came collecting money for his daughter's operation and ran back when she called to tell him she missed him.

There were, of course, the cons and the crazies — people who, *nebbach*, couldn't fit in anywhere. Like the self-proclaimed presidential candidate whose family kept him on the campaign trail for years. And the retiree who tried to turn a two-night stay into a twelve-month vacation. Rabbi Gellman smiled when he thought of how he had convinced that one to leave. After a week of excuses, it was obvious that the man just didn't want to go. So Rabbi Gellman told him that, starting tomorrow, he would be charged five dollars a day rent. By 7:00 the next morning the pensioner was out the door.

Finally, there were those whom the Hebrew Sheltering Society really ended up helping, like the man with six kids whose car broke down on the way to Pittsburgh. Trying to put six little ones to bed without disturbing the other "guests" was quite a challenge. Then there was the wealthy doctor, who could have comfortably checked into the best hotel in the city, but who stayed at the Sheltering Society, where the food and the environment were both kosher.

YES, THERE WERE A LOT of different people who lodged at the Hebrew Sheltering Society, but the Professor was certainly one of the most colorful for two reasons: first was the way he talked. Pincus boasted a florid vocabulary in English and fluency in Greek and Latin. Rumor had it that he was a former Classics professor who had suffered a nervous breakdown. But no one ever dared to find out for sure.

The second unique aspect of the Professor's personality was his self-esteem. He would become deeply insulted if it was even hinted that he was indigent, or limited in any way. The fact is that he always seemed to have enough cash to come and go as he pleased — a privilege acquired, according to hearsay, by selective borrowing from available *pushkas*. This hypothesis had as much corroboration as the one about his former occupation. But because of the Professor's lofty self-image, helping him out had its restrictions: anyone could provide him with a meal, or some sort of clothing, like a "new" used hat, but woe to the individual who merely insinuated that Pincus was in some way incapable of taking care of himself or his affairs.

Regardless of the rumors, Pincus was upright, God-fearing, didn't bother anyone, and didn't want anyone to bother him. And that is exactly what made the episode with the lawyer so strange and puzzling.

IT ALL STARTED on a Tuesday night, when the Rabbi received a call from Max, a retired tailor who served as the caretaker of the Society's house on Chestnut Street. Part of the Rabbi's responsibilities as the local spiritual leader was to administer the shelter's admissions policy.

"Rabbi, we got a new customer. His name is Jake Bernstein. He says he's a lawyer who needs a place to stay for a while. Can you stop by when you get a chance?"

"Of course," Rabbi Gellman answered. "I'll be there within the hour."

In a matter of minutes Rabbi Gellman was at the Society's headquarters to meet Jake Bernstein. Interviews of this nature were usually very brief. Papers had to be filled out and the rules of the house explained so that there would be no misunderstandings.

But one look at Bernstein and Rabbi Gellman knew he could forgo the standard explanations.

The prospective shelteree was about six feet tall, with thin brown hair and tortoiseshell glasses. In manner, in appearance and in expression, Bernstein looked every bit the dignified corporate lawyer. His cashmere overcoat had the unmistakable cut of quality that only comes from expensive clothing purchased at the "right" shops. His gray pinstripe suit was obviously tailor-made. It was all wrinkled, however. Its rumpled condition indicated to the Rabbi that the wearer had recently spent a lot of time on a train or bus.

"If you don't mind my asking," Rabbi Gellman interjected into an otherwise *pro forma* procedure, "what brings you to Scranton?"

The attorney smiled wearily, his face etched with lines formed by both physical and mental exhaustion. "I attended law school around here twenty years ago. After I passed the bar I got married, moved to Florida, and set up a practice.

"We've been married for close to eighteen years, but now my wife wants out. Just last week she filed for divorce. To tell you the truth, I was tempted to fight it to the very end. But now I feel that I shouldn't be motivated by spite. I realized that the fastest and least painful way to finish things was simply to walk away. And so, Rabbi, I left everything with her."

"I'm sorry to hear that. Our Sages tell us that the Divine Presence sheds tears whenever a marriage in Israel comes to an end. Needless to say, if I can be of assistance, please don't hesitate to ask. Max is responsible for the day-to-day operation of the house. Nadja, the Russian lady you may have seen, cooks and cleans. In the meantime, welcome, and please make yourself comfortable."

The Professor happened to be strolling down the hall and had come into the room to make sure he didn't miss anything interesting. "I overheard your tale of pain and woe, my esteemed friend, and I commiserate with you in your circumstances. I, like yourself, have been a victim of maltreatment by both individuals and institutions and have always attempted to handle my affairs in the most pragmatic manner possible. My lifetime experience is at your disposal."

"Thank you, sir," Jake smiled. "And mine is at yours."

EVERYTHING WENT SMOOTHLY the following week. Jake spent his time interviewing with different firms in the area, and Pincus spent his time "researching the stacks" at the city library.

Late one afternoon, Max was walking by Jake's room

when he heard a noise inside. Max knew that Jake was gone for the day; whoever was inside obviously knew it too.

As part of the Sheltering Society's rules, no locks were allowed on the guests' rooms. However, it was understood that everyone's privacy was to be respected. Needless to say, someone was not respecting it right now.

Quietly and slowly, Max opened the door a crack and peered in. The room was dim, but it only took a moment for his eye to adjust. From the daylight that rimmed the closed window shades, Max could make out a bent form in a long trenchcoat searching through Jake's room. It was the Professor!

"Pincus!" shouted Max as he pushed the door wide open. The Professor jumped, a startled look of guilt and shame coloring his face.

"What are you doing in here?" Max demanded.

"I... I... I was..." Pincus seemed to be frantically searching for an excuse. "I... I was looking for the attorney's newspaper," he blurted out. "It had an article on Third World economic policy and its impact on lending institutions in the U.S."

Max smiled in spite of himself and his anger. "Third World, my foot! You're looking for something else! Now, beat it! And don't even think of coming back into Jake's or anybody else's room without permission!"

"I was not thinking anything of the sort! However, I see my innocence and gilt-edged integrity are being questioned!" Pincus ad-libbed in an effort to salvage his pride. But he still looked (and felt) like a little boy who got caught with his hand in the cookie jar.

As upset as Max was, and despite his innate, long-standing aversion to Pincus, he still had compassion for the pitiful sight of the Professor. His greasy trenchcoat hung like a mantle of disgrace on his bent shoulders. "Oh God," Max invoked, "please help this man find himself."

THAT NIGHT, Max reported the episode to Rabbi Gellman. "Since I caught the Professor trying to steal, don't you think we should make him leave?" Max urged.

Rabbi Gellman thought silently for a moment. "I don't believe he wanted to take anything. I think he was simply curious."

"Curious?"

"It could be he that wanted to learn more about a man who would give up everything he had just to make peace between himself and his discontented wife."

"I'm not so sure. You know, he could take something out of Bernstein's suitcase and sell it before anyone would be the wiser. Maybe the Professor has overstayed his welcome."

Rabbi Gellman looked at him and said finally, "Let's give him another chance. In *Pirke Avos*, we find that Hillel taught, 'Do not judge your fellow man until you have stood in his place'; I've always found that to be sound advice."

THERE THE MATTER RESTED, and once again things settled into routine. According to the rules, guests were allowed to stay a maximum of two weeks at the Sheltering Society. If space was available, they could rent a room for five dollars a day after that. For Pincus, the two weeks were almost up and he couldn't afford more than a few days' rent before heading out. It was late November and the raw winds of winter were just starting to be felt. This time of year Pincus would usually try making his way as far down south as possible. That way, if he ended up sleeping on a park bench, he wouldn't freeze.

On the last morning Pincus would be able to stay at the Sheltering Society without paying, Jake came down to the kitchen as Max was sipping a cup of coffee and Nadja was washing the dishes. As she worked, she hummed a Russian folk tune. Pincus was assiduously stuffing food into his mouth and into the pockets of his trenchcoat. His duffel bag was lying on the floor, bulging at the seams with all his worldly possessions. Jake whispered unobtrusively to Max, "I have to talk to you privately."

Both men casually left the kitchen and went into the living room. Jake looked overwrought. "My cashmere overcoat is missing! I've looked all over for it and it's gone. I'm sure I left it here."

Max's eyes rolled back in their sockets. "I knew it! I just knew there'd be trouble!"

"What do you mean?" Jake asked.

"I caught Pincus in your room the other day. He was obviously searching for something. You don't think these bag-men only carry refuse and broken umbrellas in their shopping bags, do you?"

"Well, what do we do? Confront him?"

"First, I'll call Rabbi Gellman. And then..." he added gravely, "I'm calling the police."

BACK IN THE KITCHEN, Pincus sensed that the two men were talking about him. If something was wrong, he didn't want to be in the middle of it. The clock ticked away the minutes, but still Max and Jake did not return to the breakfast table. Pincus quickly finished his meal and shoved whatever edibles he could walk away with into his duffel bag. It was way too heavy to carry, so he started dragging it across the floor.

"Hold it, Pincus!" Max said sharply, striding into the kitchen. "Rabbi Gellman is on his way here to speak with you."

"What for? I have committed no crime!" the Professor said defensively.

"We'll let the Rabbi decide that!" And almost as if on cue, Rabbi Gellman walked briskly into the kitchen.

"Pincus, please come with me into the living room," he requested softly. Pincus left his duffel bag lying on the kitchen floor and followed the Rabbi.

"I assure you," he declared, "my conduct has been above reproach."

"I'm sure it has," Rabbi Gellman replied. "It's just that..."

At that moment, the sound of sirens shattered the neighborhood, wailing as though some unseen force was taking revenge upon the quiet city streets. Children from nearby houses ran to see the police car. Bicyclists pedaled out of the way, and joggers in the road hit the sidewalks mid-stride. The blue cruiser screeched to a halt just outside the shelter.

SCRANTON'S POLICE FORCE is famous for taking crime seriously and, upon occasion, overreacting. Two patrolmen-cum-detectives burst out of the front of the car, ran up the front steps and banged on the door. Max let them in and they marched into the living room with the tough, confident air that let everyone know they were capable of handling anything that might conceivably take place.

"My name is Officer Petersen. This is my partner, Officer O'Reilly. Someone reported a theft?"

"I did, Your Honor!" said Max, obviously mistaking the cop for a judge. "We have reason to believe that this man," he announced, pointing to Pincus, "stole his," pointing to Jake, "expensive overcoat!"

"That's preposterous!" the Professor protested. "I have never engaged in larceny, grand or petty, in my life. Mr. Bernstein, I wish to retain you to represent me in this case, as well as in the libel suit I intend to file against this individual," he said, pointing to Max. "And while you're at it, prepare a notice of claim against the municipality for employing such manifestly incompetent officers of the law."

"What? Let me get this straight." Jake couldn't believe his ears. "You want me," he queried, pointing to himself, "to defend you against the charge of stealing *my* coat?"

"Of course, you believe that I am not only *prima facie* innocent but also *res ipsa loquitur*. Therefore either *corpus delicti* or," he turned to the police, "*habeas corpus*."

"I don't know what to believe," a frustrated Jake interjected.

"Please, please, everyone calm down," Rabbi Gellman pleaded. By now, loud accusations were being hurled to and fro between Max and Pincus.

RABBI GELLMAN was eventually able to stop the shouting. He then turned to the two policemen, who were taking this all in with a mixture of confusion, amusement and boredom. "Officers, I'm not sure we really need your services..."

"First let's see if we can find out what's going on here," said one of Scranton's finest.

Suddenly, Pincus made a break for the kitchen. He had never liked cops and he feared that if it came down to their choosing between an employee of the Sheltering Society and him, he would end up behind bars for sure.

"Where are *you* going?" bellowed Officer Petersen. Pincus felt a strong hand clutching his arm. He managed to escape, leaving a greasy trenchcoat sleeve in Officer Petersen's hand.

Pincus tried his hardest to shuffle away with his duffel bag, but it weighed him down like an anchor. In seconds, both patrolmen had him spreadeagled against the wall. The two officers methodically frisked Pincus, searching for anything that might be used as a weapon.

"He's clean," said Petersen.

"What about the bag?" replied O'Reilly.

"Open it!" Petersen ordered.

"Where's your search warrant?" Pincus demanded heatedly. "I am fully cognizant of my rights as protected under the Fourth, Fifth and Sixth Amendments. And my attorney," he continued, pointing to Jake, "is sworn to protect them. Counselor Bernstein, would you care to recite my rights for the benefit of these perpetrators of brutality who intend to further infringe upon my constitutionally protected privileges?"

Jake tried to hide a smile. "As your attorney, and as owner of the missing coat, I think you should do as they say — or you might find yourself in custody, charged with resisting arrest, obstruction of justice, loitering, vagrancy and a half-dozen other high crimes and misdemeanors I could think of."

Pincus looked at the men surrounding him. Slowly, he upended his bulging duffel bag and watched as his world poured out in a rush. In seconds, a jumbled pile two-and-a-half feet tall spewed onto the kitchen floor.

THE ASSEMBLED WATCHED in utter awe as the officers began excavating the contents of the duffel bag: the remains of a stale tuna-fish sandwich; five maps of various cities: Passaic, Butte, Casablanca, Bakersfield and Sheboygan; a Michelin Guide; three empty potato sacks; half a dozen assorted keys; the libretto from *Cyrano de Bergerac*; four cats-eye marbles ("A little girl gave them to me for good luck"); a wad of chewing tobacco; a small pocket *Tehillim*, sans cover; an assortment of vital literature including: *The Edsel Owner Repair Manual*, *Do-it-Yourself Dry Cleaning*, *The Wonders of Afro Sheen*, and *Creative Bonsai Gardening*; a slimy banana peel; a wallet containing a complimentary pass to "The Ed Sullivan Show," a snapshot of Elvis, a folded sheet of S&H Green Stamps, and a ticket stub from *101 Dalmatians*; several pieces of string, of varying lengths, and two rubber bands, of varying elasticity; a bundle of cloth which turned out to be a long, dirty brown scarf; a dogeared *Roget's Thesaurus*; a couple of soiled shirts; a pair of suspenders; two slogan-emblazoned sweatshirts (expletives deleted); three left shoes, unmatched; a copy of *Grey's Anatomy*; a rock collection culled from suburban America; a "Rock" collection culled from decadent America (LP s); two dozen (hopefully) hard-boiled eggs; and a crumpled article from the *Times* entitled, "Third World Debt Threatens U.S. Banks."

"Quite a spread!" Officer O'Reilly said wryly. "But no coat."

"Coat? Coat? What about coat?" It was Nadja.

"Mr. Bernstein's cashmere overcoat is missing. Have you seen it anywhere?" Rabbi Gellman asked.

"Yes. It be on couch. I put in closet two days."

"I have been vindicated!" shouted Pincus. "Yet I bear no grudge against those who have cast aspersions upon my character."

"You still were caught in his room!" Max said accusingly.

"I told him he could read my *Times* when I was done with it," explained Jake.

"Excuse me fellas," Officer Petersen broke in, "but is this case solved? 'Cause if it is, we gotta go."

"Yes, officers," replied Rabbi Gellman. "Thank you for coming. We're sorry to have bothered you."

"No sweat," O'Reilly answered over his shoulder as the two patrolmen walked out shaking their heads.

MAX WAS DEEPLY ASHAMED for having blamed Pincus. He thought about what Rabbi Gellman had said about judging favorably. "I suppose I shouldn't have jumped to conclusions, Pincus. Please accept my apologies. Is there anything I can do to make up for it?"

"You're a tailor, aren't you?" asked Rabbi Gellman.

"Yes, I was one, but how does that help repair the damage I've caused?"

"You can mend Reb Pincus' coat, for a start."

"By all means," Max agreed heartily, taking the old trenchcoat in one hand and the torn-off sleeve in the other.

"And then," Pincus interjected, "you and the Rabbi could help me mend Jake's marital problems, by enabling him to see that a marriage of eighteen years' standing is worth saving."

Rabbi Gellman nodded his head as Pincus threw a solicitous arm around Jake's shoulder.

Max, gazing in awe at the pitiful mess on the floor, turned to the Rabbi and asked, "Do you think we can relax our two-week rule in this case?"

Heard from: Leibel Estrin

Labor of Love

TODAY, if you take the Romema Road in Jerusalem, cross over Kiryat Itri and wind around Rechov Sorotzkin, you'll come to Kiryat Belz. There, in between heaps of iron railings, piles of carpentry, mountains of earth, stacks of concrete slabs, and veritable quarries of Jerusalem stone, you will find a construction crew assiduously hammering, pounding, mixing, drilling, pouring, and shlepping.

This is no ordinary construction crew, and what they're working on is no ordinary construction job. The site is to become nothing less than a prominent House of God, which will be known as the Great Belzer Synagogue and Torah Center. It is being built by an elite corps of dedicated workers who observe Torah and mitzvos. To these laborers, this project isn't merely a means to earn a living; it is holy work, performed under the punctilious guidance and demanding supervision of the Belzer Rebbe himself.

When it is finally completed, the Belzer Synagogue will

be one of the most magnificent structures of its kind, not only in Israel but in the world. Built into the hills of Jerusalem on three levels it will be a city unto itself, where hundreds of Jews will spend their days and nights absorbed in spiritual activity. The synagogue will house classrooms, study halls, and *mikvaos*. In the heart of the complex will be a *beis midrash* that can hold six thousand men.

The majestic architecture and imposing design of the Great Belzer Synagogue recall a glimmer of the glory that was Jerusalem during the time of the *Beis Hamikdash*. Simultaneously, the synagogue acts as a direct link to another shul, in another place and another time: the original Great Synagogue of Belz, built almost one hundred years ago in Poland under the aegis of the first Belzer Rebbe, Reb Shalom Rokeach, of blessed memory. Its Jerusalem replica is a fulfillment of a Talmudic vision: "The synagogues and study halls of Babylonia will relocate in the future to *Eretz Yisrael*."

THERE ARE A PLETHORA OF STORIES about the original, awe-inspiring synagogue and its miracle-worker Rebbe. According to tradition, Reb Shalom was told from Above that if he studied all night for a thousand nights, he would merit a meeting with Elijah the Prophet. As this was a privilege too wonderful to forgo, Reb Shalom and two of his friends elected to attempt such an undertaking. After a few hundred nights, however, one friend dropped out. Five hundred nights later, his second friend couldn't take the strain and he, too, stopped spending the entire night learning the holy Torah.

Reb Shalom was now all alone. Night after night, he continued to study from dusk to dawn: Talmud, Halacha, Kabbala, and Chassidus. On the thousandth night, a storm broke out. The wind shrieked and howled like a denizen of the netherworld, and a terrific gust of wind shattered the windows of the old *beis midrash* into thousands of jagged pieces. Invisible hands hurled countless books all about. The lights in the oil lamps blew out and the walls vibrated from the furious, pounding crescendo of the raging storm.

Terrified, Reb Shalom made his way to the Holy Ark, which stood like a proud and loyal sentry guarding the sacred scrolls inside. He prayed fervently for help, and suddenly the storm subsided and the moon reappeared. An eerie quiet ensued and a dark apparition of an old man could be discerned standing in the shadows. We do not know what Reb Shalom heard that night from the mysterious old man, but we do know that the message pertained to the synagogue.

Not long afterwards, Reb Shalom decided to build a synagogue like no other in Galicia. Every brick, beam and shovelful of dirt and mortar would be sanctified to God. Just as the altar in the Temple served to unify and elevate inanimate objects, as well as the plant, animal and human kingdoms, so was Reb Shalom's intention in building the Great Belzer Synagogue. The Rebbe himself helped lay the bricks and performed numerous other menial jobs, which caused much consternation among those who appreciated his holiness and knew how precious every moment of time was for this *tzaddik*.

THE UNDERTAKING was accompanied by countless extraordinary events and actual miracles: like the time Reb Shalom was told that a group of merchants were passing through town. It had been raining for the last few days and work on the synagogue had slowed considerably. The dust and dirt around the construction site had turned to muck and slushy mud. Merely walking was problematic, albeit insignificant compared to the challenge of acquiring enough labor to continue the job. But Reb Shalom was not about to allow a hiatus merely for inclement weather. If the Almighty wanted the synagogue built with a modicum of *mesirus nefesh*, so much the better!

On this particular rainy day, Reb Shalom dispatched an urgent message to the merchants about to leave Belz. The *gabbai* caught the four just as they were loading up their wagon and in an obvious hurry to depart.

"*Shalom Aleichem*," greeted the *gabbai*. "Where are you gentlemen coming from?"

"Lvov. We left there several days ago, and now we're finally on our way back home to Krasnopoli," replied their leader, a heavyset cloth peddler named Moshe.

"Please, before you continue, my Rebbe would like you to take part in the mitzva of building our synagogue."

"Of course, we'll be happy to contribute something!" Moshe said magnanimously. "Here, take a few ko..."

"Oh no," the *gabbai* interrupted politely. "The Rebbe specifically invited you to help build it!"

"Does your Rebbe ask everyone who passes through town to stop what he's doing and work for him?"

"Not that I'm aware of. However, I'm sure that the Rebbe has his reasons. Shall I tell him you're coming?"

"I'd better talk this over with my companions," pondered the cloth merchant.

THE LEADER presented the Belzer Rebbe's proposal to his comrades. The response was immediate and negative. "Who does he think we are, common laborers?" demanded an indignant tinsmith named Shaul.

"We're not chassidim. What does he want from us?" grumbled Feivish, Shaul's partner.

"I've been away for two weeks! I want to get home!" exclaimed Dovid, a doleful farmer who had joined the group hoping to get a better price for his wheat in Lvov than he could in Krasnopoli.

"Listen to me for a minute!" Moshe pleaded. "Everyone knows the Belzer Rebbe is a great *tzaddik*. And is it not written, 'What a *tzaddik* does say, the Lord doth obey'? Well, if he wants us to help him, then I think we'd better do as he wishes. I'm sure he won't keep us long..."

The men looked at one another. Moshe's words struck home, especially the part about not keeping them for long.

"Instead of crossing the river in the early afternoon," Feivish calculated in an attempt to minimize the inconvenience, "we'll just get there a little later."

Moshe walked the fifteen feet or so back to where the persistent *gabbai* stood. "We'll follow you," he began, "only please tell your Rebbe that we really are very busy. We're only doing this as a favor to him."

The *gabbai* brought the men down the twisting road to where the Great Belzer Synagogue was being constructed. Reb Shalom of Belz was strenuously working alongside the few men who remained. He barely took the time to greet his reluctant employees before showing them what had to be done. "I am anxious to get the foundation finished. If you'll be kind enough to help us lay bricks, we would very much appreciate it."

THUS, THE MERCHANTS were transformed into a band of workers. Except for Dovid the farmer, it had been years since they had done any heavy labor, and the fatiguing work quickly took its toll. In minutes, Moshe's knuckles and fingers had turned into raw meat, and his soft skin was torn to shreds by rough rocks and bricks. Feivish and Shaul fared no better. While their calloused hands were accustomed to hard work, their backs weren't. As they shoveled and hoisted hefty buckets of mortar up to Moshe, it seemed as if their every muscle and tendon was being mercilessly over-stretched beyond repair. Their legs ached from standing and their toes froze from the water that had seeped in from the deluged ground. To make matters worse, the rain that had plagued their whole trip started pouring down again relentlessly.

After an hour in the downpour, which felt like a lifetime, Dovid went over to Reb Shalom and said, "We've done our share of work. Now we must be going."

Reb Shalom gave the farmer a stare that pierced his sore flesh and went all the way to the core of his being. "Please stay," he requested softly but firmly. "We have a lot to accomplish and you men are helping do a great mitzva."

Dovid gulped. One look from the Rebbe and his resistance was as depleted as his strength. "All right," he sighed, "but just for a little bit longer."

THE RELUCTANT WORKERS continued their efforts. Yet as hard as they worked, Reb Shalom worked even harder. He appeared to be everywhere at once: helping one man empty a bucket of sand, carrying bricks for another, giving instructions to a third.

After another hour, Feivish and Shaul were too exhausted to continue: panting violently, their bodies bereft of strength, racked with pain, and drenched in sweat, they collapsed on a piece of timber.

"Now I know what the slaves in Egypt felt like!" complained Feivish.

"Do you think they had it so bad?" asked Shaul.

"Why don't we just leave?" Feivish suggested to his companions. He spat at the ground disdainfully, simultaneously wiping what seemed like a cupful of sweat from his brow. "What is Reb Shalom going to do? Arrest us?"

Dovid the farmer threw a shovelful of dirt into a tub. He was as enervated as they were, but didn't want to show it. "Who knows what a Rebbe can do? Besides, I already asked him. Now it's somebody else's turn."

Shaul groaned a mighty *krechzt* as he slowly got up. "I'll try," he grunted as he made his way to where Reb Shalom was helping cut lumber. "Rebbe," he begged, "please let us go. We must reach the river before dark, especially in this rain, or we won't be able to cross it until tomorrow morning."

"What is your hurry? You spent over two weeks making money for yourselves; is two hours too much to sacrifice for a House of God? I'm sure He will reward you accordingly."

"Yes, Rebbe, we understand, but we want to leave!" Shaul blurted out.

"No one is stopping you from leaving, but if you seek a blessing you should keep on working... I'll inform you when it is time for you to go."

Shaul took a deep breath and let out a long sigh of resolve. He was used to dealing with tough customers, but never like this! "We'll do whatever you want," he promised humbly.

Retreating like a little boy aching from a parental

spanking, Shaul met his coworkers. "What did he say?" they asked.

"Uh... er... only a little while longer," he replied. "I hope," he muttered mournfully under his breath.

THE FOUR MEN continued lifting, pushing, hauling, digging and carrying. The sky began to clear and a golden-yellow sun smiled down at everyone on the site, but the foursome was oblivious to the improvement in the weather. Numbed, they performed their tasks like automatons. In his exhaustion, Feivish dropped a heavy bucket of sand on Shaul's foot. "Owwww!" cried the tinsmith. "That's it! I'm not doing another thing. Blessing or not, I've had enough!"

"It's all Moshe's fault!" Dovid chimed in, pointing to his former friend. "You're the one who agreed to this whole business."

"Yeah!" Feivish added "If it weren't for you, we would be home by now!"

Moshe was furious! He was thoroughly tuckered out, soaked with sweat and drenched with rain. And now, irony of ironies, he was being blamed for a situation he hadn't caused. He threw down his shovel and raised both his fists. "One more word from any of you and...!" But before he could finish his threat, Reb Shalom was at his side.

"You may go," the Rebbe said simply. "Thank you for your help. And may Hashem reward you generously for your efforts."

THE FOUR MEN silently stared at the ground, taking a moment to comprehend that they were now free. Each merchant exchanged glances with his colleagues as if to ask, "Can it be?" Then, as if on cue, all heads turned to Reb Shalom's departing figure for corroboration.

"Hurry, let's get to our wagon before he changes his mind," Moshe instructed conspiratorially. "We still have time to reach the river before dark."

In a lather of haste, Moshe, Dovid, Feivish and Shaul tumbled all over each other in their rush to jump onto the wagon. Moshe yanked the reins with both hands to urge his horse forward. The road was muddy but traversable, and before long they were able to put the Great Belzer Synagogue far behind them.

Ahead lay the Bug River, the last major obstacle before Krasnopoli.

THE BUG WAS FAIRLY WIDE, but there was one section where an island split it in two. A pair of rotting old wooden bridges connected both banks and from the Krasnopoli side it was only a few *versts* to town.

The sun had almost set. Moshe spurred his horse on faster. He knew that if they didn't make it to the river by dark, they'd have to come back to Belz for the night. And who knew what that might mean.

The men gritted their teeth, leaned forward and willed their wagon to accelerate. "Faster! Faster!" goaded Dovid. "It's getting late!"

"I'm going as fast as I can," Moshe shot back. "My mare isn't a racehorse, you know!"

"Shhh! I can hear water. We're almost there!" exclaimed Shaul.

The last streams of amber light were disappearing over

the treetops. The passengers craned their necks to catch the first sight of the bridge.

"I see it! I see it!" shouted Feivish. "If we hurry, we can cross before it's too late."

Moshe snapped the reins, but his horse apparently could gallop no faster. "Please, please!" he whispered to himself. "We're so close!" He snapped the reins again.

At long last, the mare picked up speed. "We're going to make it!" Dovid yelled triumphantly.

"Stop! Stop! Don't go!" a lone and unfamiliar shrill voice pierced the semi-darkness.

Oblivious to the eerie command, Moshe, determined to make his destination, drove his mare toward the wooden span.

"Get back! Stop! Get back!"

From out of the darkness, a figure half-crawled, half-stumbled toward the wagon. Dovid jumped down to help him.

"Don't go... the bridge!" he kept saying, puncturing the air with his urgent warnings.

Moshe, Shaul and Feivish ran to Dovid's side and carefully helped the stranger onto the wagon. He was shaking uncontrollably. Moshe grabbed some unsoiled cloth and wrapped it around his shoulders while Dovid held his hands.

"What happened?" Moshe asked when the man appeared coherent.

"The bridge. It looks safe, but the river rose hours ago and took the middle section away! A priest was trying to cross it and... and... he's gone!"

THE FOUR MEN looked at each other in amazement and horror, and stared back at the stranger. "I heard a scream," he continued, "then I saw him being washed away!" Then he started crying and his body shook like trees in a tempest.

Moshe, regaining his voice, turned resolutely to his companions. "My friends," he suggested, "let's take him back to Belz."

"To Belz?" asked Dovid, staring at the bridge that would have spelled their doom. "And then?"

"Then let's find the Rebbe. We have to tell him what happened. We owe him a great debt of gratitude."

"Gratitude?" asked Shaul, as uncomprehending as he was tired. "For what?"

"For saving our lives!" he responded. "If the Rebbe hadn't detained us by insisting that we stay and contribute our time to the House of Hashem, we would have crossed the riverbank much earlier and would not have met this man. Without his desperate warning, we would have surely perished in the river."

Thus having spoken, Moshe picked up the reins to lead the group back to Belz.

Who knows how many miracles will transpire in the Holy City before the new home of the Belzer Chassidim is complete? Or how many will occur before all the synagogues and study houses will be relocated in *Eretz Yisrael*?

Heard from: Leibel Estrin

Losers, Keepers

ASK THE OLD CHASSIDIM. They can tell you countless tales of the recurrent exiles and wanderings of the hidden mystic, Reb Zisha, and his holy brother, Reb Elimelech. But there is one story that they may not tell you: the one about Reb Zisha and the *sukkah*. They may not tell you because this story is scarcely known.

Early one autumn morning in the faraway Polish town of Benerov, a simple Jewish beggar tapped lightly on the door of the town's Rabbi, Reb Motke. Now Reb Motke was more than just a well-respected scholar and a pious Jew. He had a deep love for all Jews and his naturally acute powers of observation offered him a profound insight into their characters. This gift — a perceptive sense and a perspicacious eye — enabled him to discern the innermost secrets of an individual in one brief, piercing glance.

Thus, Reb Motke was not deceived by the vagabond who now stood at his front door, bending over his stick and introducing himself as Zisha, a man in need of alms. No, Reb

Motke was not taken in by Reb Zisha's pitiful garb, nor was he duped by the simple look on the man's face. Reb Motke saw in him a Jew of indeterminate age and indifferent health, trying to disguise the bright light of his soul, which shone through his modest appearance. Here, he knew at once, was someone he would be honored to have as his guest for the approaching Sukkos festival.

But when Reb Motke extended the invitation, Reb Zisha flatly declined. The Rabbi was shocked, but not dissuaded. He went on extending his invitation and Reb Zisha continued refusing. Reb Motke began to plead with the indigent to at least explain why he would not accept his offer.

The Rabbi of Benerov badgered and badgered until Reb Zisha, at the point of exasperation, finally stated, "During Sukkos I live in a *sukkah*. I don't need to be anyone's guest for the holiday."

"But every Jew," Reb Motke responded incredulously, "lives in a *sukkah* during Sukkos — at least as much as possible. All I am doing is inviting you to join us in my *sukkah*."

Reb Zisha, however, was adamant: "No, thank you," he shook his head and turned to leave.

"I don't understand what the problem is," Reb Motke called after him. "You said that you wish to live in a *sukkah* and that is precisely what I am offering you."

"But I mean *really* live in a *sukkah*," said Reb Zisha with some passion. "I sleep there, too."

"My dear friend," cajoled Reb Motke, gently guiding Reb Zisha into his home, "I don't know where your journey started, but you are now in Poland. The weather at this time of year is treacherously cold. It is hazardous to sleep in a *sukkah*."

BUT REB ZISHA refused to be swayed. He stood at the doorway and firmly repeated his sole condition for accepting the invitation. "Please, Rabbi," he implored, "on Sukkos I sleep in a *sukkah*, and that is that! I cannot accept your kind offer without this one requirement being fulfilled."

Reb Motke blocked the doorway and announced, "I am the Rav in this town." He raised his voice slightly for effect and continued, "I rule that one may *not* sleep in the *sukkah* at this time of year."

"That's fair enough," shrugged Reb Zisha, and attempted to bypass the Rabbi.

Reb Motke knew when he was bested: "All right, all right, if you insist," he said, reluctant to let such a special guest literally slip through his fingers. "What can I do? I agree to your bizarre condition. And welcome to my home."

Reb Motke was elated. He would, after all, have a chance to learn more about his mysterious visitor. And although he regretted agreeing to Reb Zisha's demand, he was convinced that the weather would ultimately persuade him to abandon his ludicrous idea.

A HOWLING STORM greeted the start of the Sukkos festival. Gritting their teeth, the townspeople of Benerov braced themselves for a holiday that would test their capacity for self-sacrifice and their determination to fulfill mitzvos under austere circumstances. *Zman Simchaseinu* was to be celebrated under a pall of frigid weather.

All over Benerov people sat shivering in their *sukkos*, clutching heavy winter coats around themselves, desperately blowing on their hands and stamping their feet trying to keep warm. Even the hearty *Yom Tov* meal they ate in the *sukkah* tasted frozen. This "happy holiday" was certainly being celebrated under the most trying conditions.

Only Reb Zisha was undaunted. When the *seudah* was over and the family had *bentched*, he nonchalantly asked his host for the bed he had been promised so that he could sleep in the *sukkah*. Reb Motke stared incredulously at his guest.

"You are being not only ridiculous," he chastised, "but a *chassid shoteh* — a pious fool! Halacha does not sanction behavior perilous to your health!"

"But Halacha does not permit one to go back on one's word either," replied Reb Zisha *sotto voce*. "I agreed to stay here under a certain condition... and now you must fulfill it."

Reb Motke was bested again. Resigned to the whims of his eccentric guest, he hauled out a bed, cognizant of the blizzard-like weather he knew would expeditiously soften Reb Zisha's determination to sleep in the *sukkah*. Just to make sure, however, he stood guard at the *sukkah* entrance, curious to see just how long Reb Zisha's obstinacy would last.

THE WIND SCREAMED and then it roared, tossing great gusts of freezing cold air all about. By now, Reb Motke, frozen at the entrance to the *sukkah*, was beginning to admire his guest's tenacity. Then, to his horror, a sudden full-force gale — or was it a hurricane — rained down ferociously on the frail *sukkah*, threatening to tear it apart and deposit the fragments beyond the Carpathian Mountains.

But Reb Zisha was not to capitulate. Standing just

outside the *sukkah*, Reb Motke overheard his guest beseech simply and quietly: "Master of the Universe, You have instructed Zisha to sleep in the *sukkah* for the seven days of the festival. With weather like this, what do You expect from Zisha? My only wish is to do as You have commanded."

No sooner had he finished his humble, impassioned plea then the *sukkah* stopped swaying in the wind. The gales continued to howl, but the *sukkah* remained untouched — an island of tranquility in a tempestuous sea. Reb Motke was dumbfounded. His earlier suspicions had been confirmed in the most extraordinary way. This man was surely no itinerant *shnorrer*. Awed by what he had seen and overwhelmed by the honor of having such a holy guest, Reb Motke meticulously catered to Reb Zisha for the rest of the holiday.

WHEN THE FESTIVAL was over, Reb Zisha thanked his host and resumed his wanderings. The Rabbi of Benerov had no way of knowing it at the time, but this was not to be a final farewell.

A few weeks after Chanukah Reb Motke was invited to the small town of Czadolia to assist the local Rabbi in a major *din Torah*. Reb Motke had never been to Czadolia before, nor had he ever met anyone from the village. The local Rabbi, proud to be host to such an important guest, graciously took him on a thorough tour of his humble town.

As they traveled along the dirt paths, Reb Motke was startled by an amazing spectacle: traversing the village square, his frail frame bent under a large sack bulging with old shoes, was the holy Reb Zisha. What made the scene most remarkable were the dozens of mocking, jeering children who followed behind him, shaking their fists and hurling the most vicious abuse at the poor man.

Stunned, Reb Motke stopped dead in his tracks. Total astonishment written all over his face, he turned to the Rabbi of Czadolia and demanded: "What is going on here?"

"Oh, he is just a simple man," replied the Rabbi matter-of-factly, not really interested in pursuing this topic of conversation. "He collects shoes that the rich no longer want or need and he distributes them to the poor."

"I wasn't referring to his occupation," countered Reb Motke, somewhat shocked, "but to the abusive way the children are treating him. Don't they realize that Reb Zisha is a *baal madreiga*?" he asked. "Someone ought to tell them!"

REB MOTKE was clearly indignant, offended that anyone would treat this holy man in such a despicable and shameful way. And in front of the local Rabbi, too! His sense of outrage, however, was not shared by the Rabbi of Czadolia.

"*Baal madreiga*?" commented the Rabbi of Czadolia scornfully. "More like a *baal aveirah*! Huh!"

He was still unmoved after Reb Motke, the revered Rav of Benerov, related the incident he had personally experienced in his very own *sukkah*. Not only was his host unimpressed, he was openly derisive.

"Everyone in this town is only too aware of the true nature of your so-called '*tzaddik*.' He has shown himself to us in his true colors! I myself have witnessed incidents," said the Rav of Czadolia. "This man stoops lower than the greediest miser, and is more corrupt than the worst government officials!" Before Reb Motke could stop him, the Rabbi had plunged into his own story to corroborate his claim:

"...It was a few years ago that the episode occurred. It was right here where we are now, in the center of town. And it happened in full view of everyone.

"I remember it was a busy market day; people had come from far and wide. Suddenly, in the middle of one of the streets leading to the market, one of the local merchants — a man well-known and respected here — broke down and started screaming uncontrollably, yelling at the top of his lungs.

"You see, he had been on his way to market with his entire life's savings in his pocket. He had planned some kind of big business deal that would have set his family up in style for the rest of their lives. 'Like clay beneath the potter's hand, thus man conforms to God's command,' it is written, and clearly God had not intended for the merchant's day to be uneventful.

"Walking toward the market, he touched his pocket to check that his money purse was still there, and — incredibly — it had disappeared! How would he marry off his daughters? How would he and his wife live in their old age? Would his wife ever speak to him again! *Oy vey* what a scene it was!

"The man promptly lost his mind. He became hysterical. His grief was so great that he simply fainted, and no one could awaken him. The entire village was gathered round as one member of the community after another tried desperately to revive him. Eventually someone produced a vial of smelling salts, which succeeded in stirring him — he even opened his eyes. But as soon as he recalled his misfortune he lost consciousness again.

"The village doctor was rushed to the scene to examine him. He pinched here, listened there, but in the end he simply shook his head. There was nothing he could do. The merchant's condition, he said, transcended the bounds of medical knowledge. We all feared for the poor man's life, and definitely for his reason. Crowds began to recite *Tehillim.*

JUST WHEN WE were at the point of despair Zisha chanced by and asked what all the commotion was about. The villagers repeated the story for him, whereupon Zisha announced that there was nothing to worry about. Pushing his way through the crowd, he approached the merchant and, shaking him with all his might, shouted that he had found the lost purse! All those around him were immediately dumbstruck with awe for Zisha.

"As for the merchant, Zisha's words worked like a magic spell. He instantly began to show signs of reviving. Slowly he opened his eyes and uttered two drowsy and incredulous words: 'You what?'

"'That's right,' repeated Zisha calmly, 'you heard me. I found your purse. But just to make sure that it's really yours, tell me, how much money did you have inside?'

"'I had exactly 10,000 zlotys,' said the merchant, who had now fully recovered his senses. 'I've counted every one of them hundreds of times. My life's savings! Oh, are you sure you have my purse?' he asked, unable to believe his good fortune.

"'Yes, yes,' Zisha nodded, 'it is definitely your purse that I have. If you come to where I am staying later this afternoon, I will be pleased to return your 9,500 zlotys.'

"'What — 9,500 zlotys!' the merchant and entire village seemed to demand in one voice.

"'Yes, of course,' said Zisha nonchalantly.

"'But there were 10,000 zlotys in the purse,' they challenged, everyone now speaking at once.

"'I am not denying that,' Zisha conceded unashamedly, 'but you must surely agree that I am entitled to 500 zlotys as a reward for my efforts.'

"AS YOU CAN WELL IMAGINE, my esteemed Reb Motke," continued the Rav of Czadolia, "the merchant didn't know what to say. The poor man was utterly exhausted by the trauma he had just experienced.

"But the villagers let Zisha have it," he emphasized, well satisfied that the story fully justified his harsh judgement of this pompous beggar imposter.

"All of the locals were outraged, of course. Since when does the finder of a lost object seek to make a profit on the mitzva? 'Have you no shame?' they censured him in disgust and indignation.

"Naturally, the knave tried to defend himself and placate the villagers. 'My dear countrymen,' he called to them. 'The fact of the matter is that I found the money, and I intend to make 500 zlotys' profit on the deal, and not a zloty less.'

"Tongues wagged, snickers abounded, and the crowd became even more heated and resentful. In the end, it was decided that I should adjudicate the dispute, which I did. But not even the aura of a *beis din* made the evil-doer contrite or even think of mending his ways. He remained absolutely adamant, insisting that he be allowed to make a profit of 500 zlotys for finding the purse. The man had not the slightest regard for the norms of decency and elementary halacha.

"It wasn't until I finally raised my voice," the Rav of Czadolia said with passion, "and stated unequivocally that there was no way according to Torah law that the finder of a lost object could keep even a fraction of it for himself, that Zisha finally acquiesced — although reluctantly to be sure.

"And so you see," concluded the Rav triumphantly, "he isn't much of a *baal madreiga* after all."

REB MOTKE did not reply immediately. He paused for a moment to allow his counterpart to calm down. He then looked the Rav of Czadolia directly in the eye and related in a soft but firm voice:

"Quite the contrary: I believe that you have misjudged the case.

"The man whose main concern today is that the poor people of Czadolia should have shoes to wear is the very same man who understood that the merchant was near death.

"The fact is, my dear colleague, that he had never really found the purse at all. Reb Zisha realized, however, that the only way to save the man's life was to restore to him his lost fortune, even if he had to do that at great personal expense.

"So you see, he concocted the entire story. He pretended that he had found the purse and he gave the merchant all the money he had at the time, raising the rest from *gemachim* and committing himself to onerous debts.

"Righteous man that he truly is, he suddenly became aware of the one dreadful drawback to what he had done:

the moment that this *tzaddik* reported his 'find,' he became painfully cognizant of the affect of his announcement on others — and on himself.

"He saw how everyone was turning towards him, their eyes filled with admiration and awe, and he blanched. He just couldn't face the envy he saw in the faces of the bystanders, envy because one Jew had been privileged with the great mitzva of saving the life of another Jew.

"With his heightened perceptions and knowledge of human nature, Reb Zisha recognized that all the admiration he was attracting could lead him to the heinous sin of haughtiness, Heaven forbid!

"Desperate, he quickly devised a way of protecting himself from that horrid evil inclination, which he knew could endanger his *neshama*. He decided to abandon his pride and incur the disfavor — even the hatred and contempt — of the villagers who had witnessed the scene.

"I can assure you that there isn't a scintilla of a *baal aveirah* in this man. His only reason for demanding a share of his fictitious find — and for going through with his charade even before the *beis din* — was his pure-hearted desire to protect himself from the sin of hubris and the townspeople from the sin of envy.

"A truer *baal madreiga* cannot be found."

Heard from: Rabbi Yosef Zeinvert

BOOK II

Introduction

THIS SECTION of *Courtrooms of the Mind* is designed for the edification and enjoyment of youngsters. It is hoped that the occasionally difficult vocabulary will serve *not* as a deterrent for young readers, but as an inducement for them to read and discuss the stories with their parents.

On the advice of educators, the themes were chosen specifically for their relevance and appropriateness for children and the stories written in a style intended to capture their attention and stimulate their imagination. As in all the other stories in this volume, the settings and periods were carefully researched and depicted as accurately as possible.

Until proven guilty

מצד מדה טובה אפילו הכף חוב הוא הרבה
יותר מכ״ז צריך לדון לכ״ז.

חפץ חיים כלל ג במ״ח סק״י

...Preferably even if the subject appears far more culpable than meritorious, one should nonetheless judge him favorably.

Chafetz Chaim Klall 3
Be'ar Mayim Chayim 10

The Benefactor's Beginning

IN THAT DARKEST and quietest hour of the night just before dawn, the solitary figure of Anshel Moses Rothschild could always be discerned making its silent way along the narrow streets of Tschortkow. In both winter and summer Anshel's footsteps were the first to mark the fresh-fallen snow or stir the dust sleeping on the shtetl's dirt roads. As the lean youth walked from his parents' home to the shul of Reb Hershel Tschortkower, he would pause at each of the village's Jewish homes, rap loudly on the door, and trumpet like the King's courier: "Arise! Arise to serve the Maker!"

Upon arriving at the Tschortkower shul, Anshel would unlock the heavy oak door, light the candles in the brass candelabrum, and kindle a small fire in the black stovepipe oven. After these initial errands came Anshel's most cherished task: he would gently kiss the velvet *paroches*, and then reach into the Holy Ark and remove the wooden box with the word "*tzeddakah*" etched on it. Only after the *pushka* was placed on the *bima* would he don his *tefillin* and then wait patiently for the others, the shtetl's *talmidei chachamim* — cobblers, tanners, milkmen and merchants — to come and complete the *minyan*.

Reb Hershel was always the next person to arrive. Upon entering, he would, as if submitting to a reflexive instinct, immediately verify that the *tzeddakah* box, which sustained the village's orphans, widows and infirm, was in its place.

REB HERSHEL had been the Rabbi of the shul and the spiritual leader of the community for many years. He gave *shiurim*, answered a steady stream of halachic questions, represented the village's Jews before the authorities, and officiated at countless weddings and funerals. Reb Hershel was also in charge of the physical upkeep of the synagogue, but when this became too strenuous for him, he asked the young and devoted Anshel Rothschild to serve as his *shammas*.

At the conclusion of davening Reb Hershel and Anshel repaired to the Rabbi's home to pursue their daily learning session. But every other Friday, even before he would open his *Gemara*, the Rabbi would first deposit the *tzeddakah* collected during those two weeks in a blue cloth bag, which in turn was hidden behind one of the many bookshelves in his study.

Over the years that Anshel worked and studied with the Rabbi, he developed a great deal of respect and admiration for the elderly scholar's erudition. He was thoroughly awed by how one person could remember so much and so readily grasp even the most difficult concepts. Indeed, whenever his Rebbe encountered a difficulty in his learning he had a remedy that always seemed to work: he would lean back in his chair, tilt his large *yarmulke* at a precarious angle, stroke his silver beard, close his sage blue eyes, and think for a few moments. When his eyes would finally open, the Rabbi would offer an explanation guaranteed to satisfy all sides of the question.

Actually the Rabbi was no less impressed by his student's gilt-edged *middos*, and he enjoyed his company immensely. What others in the shtetl derisively referred to as "naiveté," Reb Hershel recognized as Anshel's inherent integrity. In their many discussions, issues of honesty and truth seemed to be uppermost in the young man's mind, and these virtues certainly manifested themselves in his conduct.

A genuine respect and love developed between the elderly Rabbi and his young student. Reb Hershel's joy was therefore coupled with a sense of loss when he received the news of Anshel's engagement to a girl from the neighboring town of Sniaten. After his wedding, Anshel was to leave his home and the Rebbe of his youth to join his struggling father-in-law in the family business.

Reb Hershel personally oversaw the wedding preparations, contracting the most popular *klezmer* and the fanciest caterer. The ceremony and reception undoubtedly made for one of the most beautiful *simchas* ever to grace the area. The multitude of guests who arrived to bless the couple dined on fine food and delicacies and danced to spirited music until the break of dawn. Yet even as the Rabbi rejoiced with his beloved student he was simultaneously melancholic over Anshel's departure; he would never find another student and assistant like this groom.

PESACH was just ten days after Anshel's wedding and this year the trusted *shammas* would not be available to help the Rabbi with holiday preparations. Reb Hershel always mounted a very thorough search for *chometz*, including getting down on his hands and knees to peer into every corner and under every piece of furniture, and standing on top of a ladder to check every nook and cranny, shelf and drawer, and cupboard and closet of his home. This year, during the course of his inspection he discovered to his horror that the small blue bag filled with the *tzeddakah* money, a sum amounting to more than five hundred gulden, was gone!

Reb Hershel trembled. He looked behind every volume on the shelf, but it was nowhere to be found. The Rabbi then began to dismantle the bookcase, shelf by shelf, in a desperate attempt to locate the bag. Within an hour the entire house was turned upside down in Reb Hershel's fastidious search for the money he had collected for the poor.

Suddenly a thought more terrifying than the loss itself entered the Rabbi's head: only one other person knew where he hid the money. Reb Hershel tried to drive the thought away, but it kept recurring.

"But Anshel is the very personification of virtue!" he declared at last. His resolve and conviction soon wilted, however, and each attempt at vindication brought a train of condemnations in its wake.

Before long Reb Hershel found himself inadvertently rationalizing the act committed by his dear disciple: "Anshel is young, and he is also newly married. He probably needed the money to set up a home. I'm sure that he took it with the intention of returning it to my shelf later."

His mind at ease with this credible justification, Reb Hershel waited for the third day of *Chol Hamoed* before hiring a coach to Sniaten. The beauty of the journey offered the Rabbi a respite from the distress he had suffered over his lost money and his lost trust. As he traveled into the country, he forced himself to take notice of the trees just starting to bloom and the frost-bitten earth beginning to show signs of rebirth, and he hoped that maybe Anshel, too, would wish to start anew and repent.

Once in Sniaten, the Rabbi went directly to his student's new home. Anshel was overjoyed by the arrival of his distinguished guest and revered teacher, and immediately conducted him into his small, bare kitchen. Anshel served Reb Hershel tea and nuts, and inquired as to why he had merited this special visit. The Rabbi's expression turned grave and he addressed the issue directly: "Anshel, I hope you believe me when I tell you that if it had been my own five hundred gulden, I wouldn't have minded.

"I'm sure you intend to return the money bag," he continued, "and I know you had a good reason for taking it. Nonetheless," he pressed in a soft and intense tone, "it was money for *tzeddakah*, money for people who might starve without it. Therefore no one has the right to borrow from these sacred funds."

As the Rabbi spoke, Anshel grew pale and tense. The sparkle in his eyes disappeared, and beads of sweat formed on his narrow forehead. He jumped up from the table, took a jar out of the kitchen cupboard, and handed a number of coins to the Rabbi.

"It is only two hundred gulden," he said apologetically, "but I promise to return the rest as soon as I can."

The Rabbi greeted Anshel's confession and pledge with a smile and a sigh of relief. Mission accomplished, he stood up and embraced his student warmly. Anshel's eyes were swimming in tears and his shirt was wet with perspiration. Reb Hershel was also silently crying, but his tears were those of betrayal and self-castigation. "How could I have so horribly misjudged a character?" he asked himself.

For the next few months, Anshel took on side jobs in order to repay the balance of the debt expeditiously. Needless to say, both he and the Rabbi rejoiced when all the missing money was returned.

HALF A YEAR after this episode, Reb Hershel was shocked to find the village constable knocking on his door. The constable never made social visits to Jews, and the sight of him standing in the doorway, impatiently stroking the tips of his bristling moustache, was rather disconcerting. Reb Hershel immediately feared for the safety of the shtetl's Jews. "Maybe," the Rabbi thought with dread, "he is the harbinger of a new anti-Jewish decree." The officer said nothing to ease the Rabbi's fears and curtly summoned Tschortkow's spiritual leader to the local headquarters.

Upon arrival, Reb Hershel was ushered into an inspector's chamber for interrogation. "Has anything ever been taken from your home?" Startled by the question, the Rabbi blurted out the matter of the blue bag of money. But he was quick to assure the officer that all of the money had been returned by the party who had admitted to taking it.

The inspector took all of this in with supreme consternation. He then wrinkled his forehead, raised an eyebrow and fixed the Rabbi with a questioning stare as he pulled a little blue bag out of his desk drawer. "Is this yours?" he asked as he dropped the bag containing several hundred gulden onto his massive wooden desk.

At the same time, he motioned to another constable to lead in the suspect. A frail wisp of a peasant woman entered the chamber, her hands bound and her eyes on the ground. Her face was pale and drawn, and a faded red scarf covered her sandy-blonde hair. The Rabbi made a sudden and involuntary gasp as he recognized his former servant.

"Do you know this woman?" demanded the inspector.

"Ye... Yes," replied the Rabbi of Tschortkow, "she used to clean my home."

The inspector explained that one day while tidying up the Rabbi's house, the woman had happened upon the bag of money. She hid it in her apron pocket, brought it home, and buried it under a bush in her backyard.

Having inherited a small fortune overnight, the maid had quickly shed the trappings of her former existence. Daily shopping sprees became the norm, as was richly evident in her new wardrobe and well-stocked pantry.

"Eventually," the officer continued, "she quit her jobs altogether, preferring to commute to her backyard whenever she needed money. Her neighbors, however, grew suspicious of her new-found wealth and alerted us. We dispatched one of our men to monitor her activities and we arrested her a few days later. She confessed to everything.

"I really don't understand you Jews," the official stated in an analytical tone. "If this is indeed your bag of money, and if the woman's confession is true, why would someone else admit to committing the crime? You really are a queer people," he concluded. Having restored the bag to its rightful custodian, he dismissed the Rabbi with a flick of his wrist.

REB HERSHEL had as much trouble as the officer in trying to make sense out of the episode. He stroked his beard, closed his eyes, tilted his *yarmulke* at a precarious angle, and reflected on the day's events. But this time he was truly stumped, and he decided that he had to visit Anshel once again.

Contrite over the way he had misjudged Anshel, Reb Hershel prayed that he would be forgiven. He humbly knocked on his former student's door, anticipating a humiliating experience. Before the door was even fully opened the Rabbi commenced his heartfelt apology. "Please, please, forgive me," he implored. "I was so wrong to have blamed you. But what I cannot figure out is why you didn't deny taking the money?"

Anshel escorted his Rebbe into his home and explained: "When you came here on *Chol Hamoed*, I saw how pained you were over the loss of the *tzeddakah*. It hurt me so much to see your sorrowful expression. I felt that I had to do something to alleviate your grief. I realized that you wouldn't let me give you any money, so I therefore decided to acquiesce to the charge of having stolen the bag."

"I will never refer to you as my student again," Reb Hershel vowed, "for you have taught me a powerful lesson in judging others favorably." Tears welled up in his eyes as he embraced Anshel. He then blessed him: "May you always have great riches and be able to help the poor."

The Rabbi of Tschortkow removed the little blue bag and placed it in Anshel's hand. "Take this money and go to Frankfurt," he advised. "In a bigger city you will have a greater opportunity to succeed in business and to help others. Go, and may God bless you and your children for all generations."

ANSHEL MOSES ROTHSCHILD heeded his Rebbe's suggestion and departed for Frankfurt, where he became a rich merchant and banker. The Rabbi's blessing "for all generations" came to pass, for Anshel's son also became extremely wealthy, and his five grandsons settled in different European capitals, where they established a banking business that became famous worldwide. One of these grandchildren, Baron Edmond de Rothschild, known as *Hanadiv Hayadua* — "the Famous Benefactor," was always quick to point out that the prosperity of the Rothschild family stemmed entirely from the selfless generosity of his grandfather Anshel Moses.

Heard from: Rabbi Hillel David

Final Escort

PRIOR to the establishment of the State of Israel the residents of the *Yishuv* lived in dire poverty. Combining money sent from abroad with the pitiful income from their simple jobs, they struggled to eke out an existence in the Holy Land. But as difficult as life was for Jerusalemites during this era, the fate of the city's many elderly was even more heartrending. There simply weren't the financial resources to provide the care and attention that these old people so desperately needed.

It wasn't uncommon for the aged to go hungry for long stretches, and quite frankly, many of the local residents were too preoccupied with their own financial hardships and wondering how they would feed their families to worry about the needs of senior citizens.

There was, however, one person who made the plight of the elderly his foremost concern. His name was Rabbi Eliyahu Reichman and he served as the secretary of Jerusalem's old age home. Reb Eliyahu had assumed a heavy responsibility, for the residents of the home were totally reliant upon him for their sustenance.

Reb Eliyahu's selfless acceptance of this duty earned him a reputation for being one of the righteous men of the old *Yishuv*. Such a reputation wasn't easily acquired at a time when even the simple tinsmiths and humble cobblers were pious, learned individuals.

The key to his success was his method of soliciting funds. His soft words and honest pleas melted hearts to the point that whomever he met actually looked forward to parting with their meager income in order to keep Jerusalem's old age home running. Whenever they saw the furrowed forehead, gaunt cheeks and silver-gray beard of Reb Eliyahu approaching, they knew that some sort of pledge, no matter how small, would be courteously elicited.

Providentially, Reb Eliyahu was joined in this line of work by his closest friend, Reb Shlomo Katz. Actually, raising funds for the infirm and elderly of Jerusalem was just one of the many interests these two shared. They had learned Torah together from the time they were children, and had grown up side by side in the *Yishuv* under the most austere conditions. Small wonder their friendship could not be accurately described with trite clichés like "brotherly love" and "genuine comradeship." For well over sixty years they intuited each other's thoughts and feelings, sharing life's joys and halving its sorrows. There was nothing one would not, or could not, do for the other.

NEEDLESS TO SAY, one of the greatest sorrows Reb Shlomo ever suffered was the passing of his friend and brother Reb Eliyahu. Reb Shlomo was joined in his mourning by countless residents of Jerusalem, who were heartbroken by the bitter news. Reb Eliyahu had touched and helped so many people, and they all came together to express their grief at the tragedy.

It was a gloomy day; the sky was gray and bleak, and there was a sharp nip in the air. It seemed as if even the weather had been tailored to reflect the mood of the people, for the atmosphere was thick with sadness. Nonetheless, inclement weather could not deter the untold hundreds of men and women from this final act of *chessed* for Reb Eliyahu.

Streets began to swell with mobs blocks away from the site of the funeral. The crowd jammed the cramped, winding roadways converging on the main thoroughfare along which Reb Eliyahu's body was slowly carried. Groups of mourners desperately tried to join the funeral procession, a sea of black in which masses of people dressed in Jerusalem's traditional garb pressed tightly together, wherever they could. All along the route were scores of women, children, and those too infirm to walk. Peering through the arched windows of the single-story and double-story stone structures were many of the aged who had benefited directly from the deceased.

SHEPHERDING this slow-moving flock was the bereft Rabbi Katz. Reb Shlomo had never looked more alone than he did on that day. Watching the grief-stricken figure trudge behind the body brought rivulets of tears to those participants keenly aware of the deep friendship that had existed between the two. The abundant sorrow over Reb Eliyahu aroused equal emotions of compassion and sympathy for Reb Shlomo's suffering. But these feelings were suddenly shattered into fits of indignation when Rabbi Katz abandoned the funeral to enter a flower shop.

It was the most bizarre and poorly timed act imaginable! Many stopped in their tracks in disbelief, their eyes riveted to the flower shop, silently hoping for an explanation for such ignoble behavior. But Reb Shlomo was not to be exonerated, for a few minutes later he emerged with a potted plant in his arms, and headed in the opposite direction of the Mount of Olives cemetery.

People from all walks of life had gathered to pay their final respects, and in some small way repay the kindness to a man who had graced their city with so much benevolence. But all of a sudden the focus of the funeral shifted to murmurings about the deceased's supposed best friend. "Couldn't he have waited one more day before buying his plant?" the crowd grumbled reproachfully.

REB SHLOMO'S BEHAVIOR even disturbed the gentle, kindly soul of one of the most respected *tzaddikim* in Jerusalem, Rabbi Leib Levy. Instead of harboring his shock, however, he realized that he was obliged to rebuke and correct the sinner. Does not the Torah instruct, "You shall not hate your brother in your heart; you shall surely admonish your neighbor..."? To avoid hard feelings, Reb Leib confronted Rabbi Katz right away.

"I simply cannot understand your behavior," he chided softly, clasping both his hands. "Please correct me if I am wrong, but weren't you the *niftar*'s closest friend for over six decades? Where is your respect and honor for the deceased? How could you abandon him to purchase a flower pot?"

Reb Shlomo couldn't be offended by Reb Leib's question, for he was a good enough student of human nature to realize that there was bound to be strong criticism regarding his seemingly outrageous conduct. He gently took Reb Leib's arm and started to walk with him down the street.

"Reb Leib," he began, "I do not mean to detour you from the funeral but I cannot be delayed. You see, for years I have been visiting a leper in the hospital. Yesterday he passed away and his gentile doctors ordered that all of his possessions, and anything that had come in contact with him, be incinerated.

"I immediately feared for his *tefillin*. I knew that his doctors would not make any exception for them, but I had to try and save them from being burned. After I explained the matter to one of the doctors, he agreed to allow me to bury the *tefillin*. He stipulated, however, that I must bring a flower pot to the ward today before noon if I had any intention of sparing them.

"From the time that Reb Eliyahu was summoned to the Heavenly Court I have been guarding the body, and have had no other opportunity to take care of this matter. I hope you will trust me when I tell you that knowing Reb Eliyahu the way I did, I believe that had he been faced with the same situation — and you know that there was no limit to what he would do to help someone in distress — he would have acted in the exact same way."

Reb Leib nodded his head and understood that no one would have preferred to escort the *niftar* to his final resting place more than his closest friend. Wiping away a wistful tear he commented, "May I resolve today to always give people the benefit of the doubt and may we all be comforted among the mourners of Jerusalem."

Reb Leib then turned to hurry back to the funeral. He was anxious to request that Rabbi Eliyahu Reichman beseech the Almighty to judge all of *Klal Yisrael* favorably.

Heard from: Rabbi Shlomo Zalman Auerbach

Wrong Prognosis

WHEN CHAIM AND TZIPPY KLEIN moved to Toronto in 1976 they were barely noticed among the hundreds of others who came that year. Toronto annually attracts scores of families who seek to live in a young, affluent, religious environment. Centered on prime real estate on Bathurst Street, Toronto's Jewish community is amongst the most flourishing in North America.

The influx of Jews is actually not all that different from the overall demographic growth in the area. The city's prosperity draws a third of Canada's 150,000 annual immigrants. From the farm-gobbling suburbs in the east and west, and from the underdeveloped north, droves of men and women flock to Canada's center of finance, education, and the arts.

1976 was the year of the great Jewish immigration. Seeking neither the social services nor the culture that Toronto is famous for, neighbors from the eastern province of Quebec migrated for political, and ultimately religious, considerations. After months of debate, compulsory French-language education had been legislated throughout Quebec. The yeshivos would have to instruct in French or close down, a hardship not even known in Rashi's France. This decree and other ethnocentric measures that Montreal Jews feared would come in its wake sent many families packing to the industrial capital of Ontario. *C'est la vie*!

With so many people moving in, the usual warmth and hospitality associated with Toronto were necessarily spread thin. Chaim and Tzippy were surprised at the curt welcome offered by the tenants of their multi-story apartment house. Their building, like many of the other tall apartment complexes on Bathurst Street, was inhabited almost exclusively by Jews, yet even their next-door neighbors did not extend more than a brief visit of the welcome wagon. That is why Dr. and Mrs. Miller's reception of the Kleins made such an indelible impression on them.

DR. MILLER was a sixty-eight-year-old retired pediatrician who spent part of his day learning, and the other part of it practicing what he learned. He was complemented by Naomi Miller, his faithful assistant and loving spouse.

The Millers kept a keen eye focused out their window. They were forever on the lookout for any mitzva that might fall within their domain, and the sight of a moving van unloading household furnishings directly across from their house was a Godsend.

The elderly couple phalanxed into action with the zeal of a teenage twosome. Chaim and Tzippy were promptly invited for supper that night, for the upcoming Shabbos, and for any other meal in between. Dr. Miller recited for Chaim the times and places of the *minyanim* on the block, while his wife detailed the shopping centers to her counterpart.

By virtue of sheer geography, the Kleins were obvious targets for the Millers' magnanimity — they lived directly across the street. The fact that the newlyweds' apartment was on the fifth floor must have been an inconvenience for the senior citizens — but one would never have known.

True, they used the elevator for their weekday pilgrimages, but on Shabbos they were not deterred from scaling the staggering 110 steps to be with their young friends. Not dependent upon invitations, Mrs. Miller could often be seen hauling up a basket of cinnamon buns or other goodies, which she feigned she didn't know what to do with. On practically a daily basis, Tzippy would hear how Mrs. Miller "just happened to be in the neighborhood." Shabbos visits were devoted to discussions and sound advice that the sagacious doctor shared with his across-the-street-and-up-the-stairs neighbors.

The close relationship forged between the two couples could have led any outsider to assume that Chaim and Tzippy were actually the Millers' daughter and son-in-law. There may not have been a resemblance, but the attachment was uncanny.

For their part, the Kleins tried to return the gesture, but they had neither the grace nor the *savoir-faire* of those much their senior. They were also not well-seasoned in the art of sharing with others, yet they were learning. The Kleins' greatest handicaps were their youth and inexperience. For a relationship to last it must be a reciprocal one. And although the Millers disdained the little errands and chores performed by the Kleins on their behalf, they permitted them for the sake of the friendship.

An obvious by-product of this relationship was the trust the Kleins placed in the Millers. The young couple took the Millers into their confidence in all realms of life. Soon, there was little the Kleins did — in terms of dealing with neighbors, in terms of treating others with loving kindness and in terms of leading a *frum* lifestyle — without previously consulting with the Millers.

THE MECHANICS OF MITZVA FULFILLMENT require a great deal of caution. A small miscalculation, an error in timing, or an improper measurement can result in the violation or non-fulfillment of numerous Torah commandments. Hence constant meticulousness and a profound sense of responsibility accompany each decision made by an individual in the realm of religious observance. For this very reason some avow strict allegiance and adherence to spiritual leaders in all halachic matters, in order to feel confident that they are properly fulfilling their obligations. Thus, if one discovers that the *kashrus* standards of a long-patronized butcher are unsatisfactory, there is minor comfort in the fact that one had previously investigated the issue with a rabbi who had given his approbation.

In many ways the Millers filled this authoritative role for the Kleins. Dr. Miller was a learned man well-versed in Toronto's religious infrastructure. He knew whose chicken or *mezuzah* was reliable, and whose rabbinical supervision was acceptable. All of this information was discreetly passed on to Chaim and Tzippy.

Relying on Dr. Miller made the young couple's adjustment all that much easier and quicker. The Millers were the Kleins' religious advisors... until one fateful Shabbos afternoon, when a thicket of suspicion sprang up between them.

The Millers had concluded their regular Shabbos visit to the Kleins and were heading home. Tzippy looked out the window to watch them cross Bathurst, when suddenly her eyes filled with horror. Chaim, hearing his wife's throttled gasp and seeing her ashen expression, ran to the window to see what the problem was.

They were both stupefied. They stared in silent disbelief as Dr. and Mrs. Miller slowly climbed into a taxi. As much as they wanted to, judging favorably was beyond their ken. What medical excuse could warrant such a brazen violation of Shabbos? They had just seen the Millers and found them full of stamina and health. Possessing no evidence of a life-and-death situation, the Kleins painfully concluded that the Millers were not Sabbath observers.

Chaim and Tzippy thought of confronting them, but every imagined interaction inundated the young couple with a deep sense of embarrassment, betrayal and fear.

The Kleins summarily put a freeze on their relationship with the kind and friendly Millers, and the older couple immediately sensed the chill. They understood that their presence was no longer desired, and they gracefully refrained from pursuing their usual feats of neighborliness — no questions asked.

The Millers had other mitzvos to look for and fulfill and new people to latch onto. The Kleins were confident that they themselves were established enough in the neighborhood and city to fend for themselves. The lives of the two couples went on, in parallel lines that did not meet.

LATE THAT WINTER the tragic news of Dr. Miller's death came to the Kleins' attention. Tzippy and Chaim were ashamed that they had missed the funeral and came so late in the *shiva* to be *menachem avel*.

Their visit was, as could be expected, a bit awkward. They hadn't been in the Miller home ever since the taxi incident in the late spring. But their feelings of betrayal and of being misguided by the Millers quickly melted when they saw Mrs. Miller's devastated, hollow look.

From their distant corner in the crowded living room, Tzippy whispered to Chaim that perhaps they had been too rash in severing their ties with the Millers. Her husband was quick to correct her, however, and put things in their proper perspective.

"If not for the passing of Dr. Miller, and the fact that we now have to reenter his home, you would still feel the same way I do. They gained our trust under false pretenses. True, they were very hospitable and everyone gained from their *chessed*, but *mechallelei Shabbos befarhesia* are hardly the people we want as confidants and advisors."

Tzippy concurred, but somehow her uneasiness was not assuaged. She and Chaim dutifully moved forward as others in the room got up to leave. Soon they found themselves all alone with the bereft Mrs. Miller, and the silence in the room was resounding.

Chaim sought the most neutral and impersonal conversation possible under the circumstances. "We were so sorry to hear the terrible news. How did your husband pass away?"

Mrs. Miller took a deep, shaky breath and looked straight at the Kleins. "He had a massive heart attack," she replied.

"Did he have a history of heart disease?" Tzippy blurted out, hoping that a more clinical topic would steer the talk away from their old relationship.

"Oh yes," Mrs. Miller said somberly, "his first attack was in the late spring... as a matter of fact it was on a Shabbos, as we were walking down the stairs from your apartment.

"Since my husband was a doctor he recognized the early warning signals, and we immediately got into a taxi and sped to the hospital..."

Heard from: Sussy Brecher

Weighs and miens

❦

ואפילו במקום שהכף חוב מכריע יותר דמצד הדין ליכא איסורא כ״כ אם יכריעהו לכ״ח היינו לענין שיוסכם בעיני עצמו עליו שעשה שלא כדין אבל אין למהר לילך ולבזותו עבור זה אצל אחרים...

חפץ חיים כלל ג:ח

And even in a situation where Halacha permits one to judge unfavorably, this is only regarding one's personal opinion; however, one may not take the initiative of shaming the subject before others...

Chafetz Chaim Klall 3:8

Parsimonious Patronage

THERE REALLY WEREN'T too many places to find extra cash in Jewish Cracow. As each Jew eked out his meager living, any money left over after expenses was usually taxed by communal organizations such as the shul and the *mikve*. But the Jewish residents of Cracow did not object to the taxes, for they realized the importance of a strong *kehillah*.

The backbone of the community was the rabbi, a God-fearing scholar named Reb Zundel. In Cracow, Reb Zundel's word was law. No one ever questioned his authority or argued with his decisions. Indeed, his counsel was sought in all matters, and his skill at arbitration was frequently utilized.

But even the saintly Reb Zundel could not bring his influence to bear upon the richest — and stingiest — Jew in all of Cracow, Shia Hershowitz, known to one and all as "Shia the *Kamtzan* (miser)."

Clearly half of the community lived below the poverty

line, and a large portion of that group actually went hungry. In Cracow, there was never a halachic dilemma on Purim as to who was eligible to receive *mattanos le'evyonim.*

But Shia the *Kamtzan* was unmoved. A man of enormous wealth, he had no intention of sharing it with others. He wouldn't even lend a sympathetic ear to the neediest causes. It was no surprise, then, that he was despised by every Jew in the city.

People of Shia's means, even niggardly ones, will occasionally dole out a little money here and there. They will make a large donation for the sake of their personal public relations: to ensure that their children marry well, or that they will not be remembered as total scoundrels. But not Shia the *Kamtzan*.

ONE SUNDAY AFTERNOON, word went out that Shia the *Kamtzan* had become seriously ill and was not expected to live for more than a few hours. The news was greeted with mixed reactions. Those who had personally approached him for money and were refused were not ashamed to express glee over the tidings. Many others, however, felt that this was a golden opportunity for Shia's — and their own fortunes — to take a turn for the better.

Long lines formed outside the miser's home in the hope that now, when the end was manifestly near, Shia would feel contrite and would desperately try to "buy" himself a place in Heaven. Even the venerable Reb Zundel was summoned to make the most of this chance. The more prestigious members of the community argued that the Rabbi should be the town's representative in asking Shia for a substantial donation to the poor. Others contended that it would be best for Shia to receive hundreds of solicitations. Seeing so many penniless people, they hoped, might soften his hard heart. Both sides agreed that they had to act fast, for who knew how much longer Shia the *Kamtzan* had left on this Earth.

To the frustration and shock of all, incorrigible Shia the *Kamtzan* would not even relent on his deathbed! Poor people cried at his bedside for just a few kopecks, though the loss of a thousand rubles wouldn't have made a dent in his fortune. But Shia was determined not to share with others.

As Reb Zundel neared the sick man's room, the impoverished townsfolk suggested, "Shia is probably not Jewish. Doesn't the Talmud say that benevolence is an inherent characteristic of a Jew? This *kamtzan* exceeds all norms of stinginess! Don't lower your dignity, Rabbi; don't waste your time with a *sheigetz*!"

REB ZUNDEL suspected that they might be right, but he had to give Shia a chance. He entered the room and observed that the man was in a deathly state. Remarkably, however, the great nay-sayer was neither cantankerous nor bitter.

Reb Zundel showed concern for Shia's condition, and then began to exhort him regarding the end of life. "In the end," the Rabbi emphasized with strong conviction in his voice, "one takes only good deeds to the other world. All material possessions will have to remain behind."

But Reb Zundel's impassioned plea was futile. He serenely wished the Rabbi well but told him to abandon his appeal, and to convey this message to all of the others waiting outside for a handout.

Defeated, Reb Zundel turned to leave, but Shia called him back. Yet instead of repenting, as the Rabbi thought he would do, he merely reached over to his night table, removed a piece of paper sealed with wax, and handed it to the Rabbi. Reb Zundel, however, was in no mood to discover the miser's intent. He stuffed the paper into his pocket, and exited to an anxious crowd of townsfolk eager to hear how their Rabbi had fared. The Rabbi's facial expression said it all, and a noisy chorus of "You see," "I told you so," and "What did you expect?" erupted from the mob.

DISAPPOINTED, BUT NOT SURPRISED, the poor Jews of Cracow plodded home. The members of the *chevra kadisha*, however, refused to leave. They believed that they possessed the grim aura of finality that no human, not even Shia the *Kamtzan*, could withstand.

Four members of the *chevra kadisha* walked into Shia's room and announced, "We have not come to beg. We have come to inform you that if you do not sign over four thousand rubles to the *gabba'ei tzeddakah* of Cracow right now, we will not bury you. We shall see that your remains never desecrate our cemetery."

"So be it," responded Shia, and with those words his soul expired.

The *chevra kadisha* had every intention of carrying out their threat, and they knew that there would be no one to champion the late miser's cause. "Let him rot," they snickered, "as he allowed us to rot in poverty." With the ease of forgetting yesterday's toothache, Cracow put aside all thoughts of Shia the *Kamtzan*.

LATE THURSDAY NIGHT, Tuvia the cobbler knocked repeatedly on the Rabbi's door. "Reb Zundel," he pleaded, "I don't know where else to turn. I have beseeched all the *gabba'ei tzeddakah* in town, but they refuse to give me any money or even grant me a loan. What am I to do? Tomorrow night is Shabbos and we don't even have a kopeck."

The learned Reb Zundel was moved by Tuvia's plea. "Come inside," he beckoned. The Rabbi served the cobbler a cup of tea and handed him two rubles. "*A gutten Shabbos*," he blessed Tuvia, and escorted him to the door.

Early the next morning Reb Zundel was awakened by Gittel the seamstress. "Oh Rabbi," she begged, "you know that I still have five children at home... and I have no way of making Shabbos."

Reb Zundel looked at the frail woman and was struck by her utter desperation. "Did you approach the *gabba'ei tzeddakah*?" he asked kindly.

"Of course I tried; everyone has tried. But they say that there is no money left."

Reb Zundel was puzzled. The *gabba'ei tzeddakah* were fair and extremely cooperative. But even more confounding was Gittel's assertion that "everyone has tried." The Rabbi wanted to question her about it, but he feared that in her worrisome state, she could not be expected to offer a comprehensible answer.

Reb Zundel had only three rubles left in his house. He also needed money to prepare Shabbos for his own family, but how could he refuse this destitute widow? He went to his bureau, removed a ruble and a half, and graciously handed the coins to the woman, wishing her "*A gutten Shabbos*."

REB ZUNDEL was confused and concerned. Although he knew that Tuvia and Gittel had trouble making ends meet, they had never approached him before.

In fact, none of the numerous poor people in town had ever approached him for help. And now, even before davening he could see two beggars nearing his home.

Both indigent souls told the same story: they hadn't the means to make Shabbos, and they were out of ideas, after having tried all the other possibilities. He apologetically sent them away with half a ruble each and a half-mumbled Shabbos blessing.

"Could this be a test engineered by local critics?" the Rabbi wondered. There had to be some explanation, some reason why all of a sudden poor men and women, people who never turned to the *gabba'ei tzeddakah*, were all out of money on the very same day.

On the one hand, Reb Zundel did not wish to interrogate these charity cases; after all it was a privilege to give to the needy. But on the other hand, he had to solve this mystery. The Rabbi decided to question the next person who sought his aid; and he didn't have to wait for long... Gimpel the bagel baker was shuffling sadly to Reb Zundel's house.

"Rabbi," Gimpel began, "I have already made my deliveries for Shabbos, yet I do not have enough money to provide for my family. Please help me, I have tried everywhere and do not know where else to turn."

"Tell me, Reb Gimpel," the Rabbi said in a soothing tone, "is this the first time that you have been short of cash?"

"Well... it is the first time in many years."

JUST AS GIMPEL WAS ANSWERING, Laibel the pompous wagon driver rapped on the front door. Although he was a very proud man, it was a well-kept secret that Laibel was actually a poor one as well. He wore tall, polished boots and enjoyed strutting around town waxing his handlebar moustache. Perched on top of his wagon he was wont to give the impression that he was sitting on top of the world.

But for once Laibel looked downcast. Even the polish on his boots seemed dull in the morning light.

"Laibel, what's the problem?" the Rabbi asked, quickly opening the door and escorting him inside.

Laibel, with a broad chest and an ordinarily booming voice, answered in a barely audible tone: "I don't have any money for Shabbos, and I simply cannot face my wife like this. She thinks that I am the richest man in the world. What am I to do?"

"Tell me, Reb Laibel," the Rabbi said, trying to calm down a very anxious soul, "did you ever have money problems like this before?"

"NO! Well... not for years."

THE RABBI REALIZED that if Gimpel or anyone else were to spot Laibel in his house and guess the reason for his visit, the wagon driver would be mortified. He therefore ushered him into the innermost room in his house, excused himself, and resumed his discussion with Gimpel.

By the time Reb Zundel returned, Gimpel was a nervous wreck. "Rabbi," the poor bagel baker pressed, "Shabbos is in another nine hours, and we don't have money to buy even a small fish for the meals."

"Don't worry," the Rabbi responded as calmly as he could. Reb Zundel did not know how he would provide for all of the city's poor, but he understood all too well that he had to discover the cause of this sudden, widespread deprivation immediately.

"Tell me," the Rabbi continued "how have you managed to get by until now?"

"With the envelope."

The Rabbi looked confused. "The envelope?"

"Yes, of course. Early every Thursday morning a white envelope containing seven rubles was slipped under my door."

THE RABBI WAS AMAZED. Just as he was about to ask for details, there was another knock on his door. It was Shifra, the city's most active *gabbais tzeddakah*, waiting with a frantic expression.

"Rabbi," she began, not even pausing for a word of greeting, "there is total bedlam in this city. Hundreds of poor people are clamoring at my door and the doors of the other *gabbaim*; they're desperate for money to make Shabbos. This has been going on since early Thursday and by 9:00 in the morning we had all run out of money.

"I tried to make an appeal, and personally knocked on the doors of some of the richest people in town, but their homes were already swarming with beggars seeking a few kopecks. Rabbi, you had better do something fast before this turns into a major calamity, Heaven forbid!"

THE RABBI had every intention of doing something and was about to suggest a plan when he was startled by a noise coming from the back of his house. He asked Shifra to wait for him while he raced to the rear of his home, only to find Laibel bawling like a baby.

"Oh Laibel," the Rabbi consoled, removing a handkerchief from his pocket and dabbing the grown man's cheeks, "everything is going to be all right. By the way," Reb Zundel interjected, "how did you manage until now?"

"Every Thursday morning," the burly wagon driver whimpered, "five rubles in a white envelope were stuffed under my door."

The Rabbi was agog. "Tell me," he asked, determined to learn more about these envelope episodes, "were you ever in financial need before you started receiving the envelopes?"

"I was, but it was many, many years ago. What does it matter now?" His last words were dissolved in tears.

Reb Zundel left him sobbing and returned to Shifra.

"IF YOU HAVE ANY DOUBTS about the dimensions of our problem," sighed Shifra, "look who's coming to see you now."

Down the road about a dozen more beggars were making their way to the Rabbi's house.

Trying to keep a note of desperation from his voice, the Rabbi asked Shifra if she knew anything about envelopes that had been slipped under the doors of the indigent.

"Until yesterday morning I didn't," she admitted. "All of these people claim that the envelope deliveries weren't made this week and they have no way of managing without them."

"For how long have these envelopes been distributed?"

"Each person has a different story, but by and large they have been receiving them for quite a number of years."

"I suggest the following," Reb Zundel recapitulated. "While I try and solve the envelope riddle, you go back to town with those who have come here and proclaim in my name that every Jewish resident of Cracow is to donate whatever funds he can to his poor brethren. Since there will still not be enough money to go around, I enjoin all the townspeople to share the food they have prepared for Shabbos with the needy. This way we will all be able to manage, and no one will, God forbid, go hungry this Shabbos. My Rebbetzin is shopping in town now; instruct her that I want her to oversee the food-sharing operation."

Reb Zundel then returned to his detective work, buttonholing Gimpel.

"My old friend," he wheedled, "when did you last have a money problem like this?"

"Many years ago, even before you became the Rabbi."

"What did you do about it?"

"I went about asking for help."

"Whom did you turn to?"

"Well at first, like every other poor person in Cracow, I turned to the wealthiest man in town, Shia the *Kamtzan*. You know, the man who died this week."

"What did he say to you?"

"Well, at first he was rather cordial, and he even looked a little concerned. But I should have known better."

The Rabbi shook his head in understanding.

"He asked me a battery of questions: what I do, the amount that I earn, how many children I have, where I live, how much money I need, and so forth. The whole time he was asking me these questions, I was sure that he was deciding on a specific sum to give me. And then — the *chutzpah* of that filthy-rich *kamtzan* — he told me to leave and to never come back again.

"I walked out of there with my heart in my mouth, cursing the old miser. And let me tell you, Cracow is a lot better off now that he is gone!"

"So, then, how did you get your money?" the Rabbi persisted.

"I tried asking some other rich people. They said they couldn't spare more than a kopeck or two at the time, but at least they didn't throw me out of their homes. They told me to try again around *Yom Tov*. Anyway, the envelopes started arriving on a regular basis that Thursday and they never stopped... until yesterday."

REB ZUNDEL thanked Gimpel for answering his questions and informed him regarding the food-sharing plan. "I hope that by next Shabbos," he concluded, "a better system will be worked out."

The Rabbi then went to Laibel, who was still sitting with his head in his hands.

"Reb Laibel," cajoled the Rabbi, "when you had your financial difficulties years ago, how did you go about easing them?"

"*Oy*," moaned Laibel, "don't even make me remember that time. Second only to today it was the most humiliating day of my life."

"I'm sorry," the Rabbi continued, "but I must know what occurred."

"Well, if you insist... I was told to seek out the richest Jew in all of Cracow, Shia the *Kamtzan*. I had heard that he didn't part with his money so I was afraid even to appeal. But as time went on, I saw that I had no alternative. Only in sheer desperation did I finally approach him.

"Was that a mistake! Here he listens to my whole story, and asks me questions and particulars about my family, my street, and how much money I need. He made me think that he was really going to help, and in the end he tells me to get out of his house and never return. Do you think I feel the least bit sorry for him now that he's dead?"

"So, how did you manage?" Reb Zundel interrupted.

"Well, the next day, it was a Thursday, I found an envelope under my door filled with just the amount of money I needed. This has been happening every week, until yesterday, for the last nine years."

At this point, the Rabbi began to cry uncontrollable tears. "Woe is me," he wailed, "woe is me! Woe to all of us, woe to the city of Cracow! Holy, holy Shia, please, won't you ever forgive us!"

Laibel didn't understand what was happening. The Rabbi turned to him and asked if his wagon was available. Laibel nodded his head, and the Rabbi asked to be driven to town at once.

On the way, the Rabbi suddenly remembered the sheet of paper Shia had handed him just before he died. Reb Zundel reached into his pocket and nervously broke open the seal. Inside was a simply worded will bequeathing Shia Hershowitz's entire fortune to the poor of Cracow.

AS SOON AS THEY ENTERED the crowded town square Reb Zundel stood up in the wagon and proclaimed in a loud, cracked voice: "Attention Jewish residents of Cracow, in exactly one hour will be the funeral for the holy Reb Shia, the greatest *baal tzeddakah* this town has ever known. Everyone — without exception — is to attend and beg his forgiveness!

"Whom do you think placed the white envelopes on your doorsteps for years and years, bearing your contempt for him in order to spare you the humiliation of having to go scrounging each and every *erev Shabbos*? May Hashem forgive us all for our ugly words and thoughts.

"This secret *tzaddik* who preferred scorn to adulation must be publicly honored by all of his many beneficiaries."

The shamefaced *chevra kadisha* meticulously dressed the body of Reb Shia, a body which had remained remarkably fresh, in a pure white *kittel*. And in this white envelope Reb Shia was laid — without anonymity — at the doorstep of God.

Heard from: Rabbi Yosef Zeinvert

Reflections

A SEA OF BLACK rolled in with the Rebbe as he approached a well near the seashore. It was a special day for Belzer chassidim. Every year on this date, the day before Passover eve, the Rebbe's devoted followers would tear themselves away from their Pesach cleaning in order to join their master as he drew the water that would be used on the morrow for the baking of matzos.

Reb Aharon Belzer had started a tradition of telling a story at the site of the well, and it was no secret that the chassidim loved to hear him spin a tale.

The occasion was also an opportunity to consult with their spiritual mentor and raise their most detailed and penetrating questions. Aside from receiving a private audience with the Rebbe, his followers really had no other way to approach him. On *Yom Tov*, as at a *tisch*, the Rebbe was a king ensconced on his throne, busily surveying his subjects and dispensing public counsel, blessings, and *shirayim* (food).

When they had arrived at the well one of the chassidim approached the Rebbe and asked, "Every year the Rebbe blesses us that we should be privileged to bake *matzos mitzva* in *Yerushalayim* the next day. But venerable Rebbe, have we not learned that the Messiah — who will shepherd us back to *Yerushalayim* — will not come on either a Shabbos, Friday, or holiday eve? The Rebbe's annual blessing appears to contradict this dictum."

Reb Aharon heaved a sigh and responded, "Eliyahu Hanavi, who will herald the arrival of the Messiah, will solve all of our perplexing questions, this one as well." He then added* with a twinkle in his eye, "If we see Eliyahu tomorrow I'm afraid that we will be so busy preparing our *Korban Pesach* and *matzos mitzva* that we may not get a chance to ask him ..."

The chassidim understood from the way the Rebbe had concluded his quip that he was ready to weave a tale. They knew that their Rebbe would relate a fascinating story which would add meaning to the approaching holiday and enrich them throughout the whole year.

The Rebbe lowered his bucket into the well, and then turned to his followers with these words:

"There is a tale about a Jewish couple and their urgent problem, but its message is for every one of us..."

THE LITTLE TOWN of Shpaltov had a dedicated spiritual leader, a Rabbi who, in many ways, was overqualified for his position. Shpaltov had never had such

* As related in *Admorei Belz*.

a learned Rabbi before, and his erudition was matched by a genuine concern for others. To a great extent both of these attributes were lost on the simple townsfolk. Their level of education did not enable them to appreciate his scholarship, and they considered the Rabbi's ideas about reaching out and affecting every Jew in the area impractical.

Several of the villagers justified his behavior with mock sympathy. "What else could you expect from the poor Rabbi?" they would cluck. "He doesn't have, *nebbach*, anything else to do."

They were alluding to the fact that the Rabbi was not blessed with children. His sad plight was often talked about, but gone were the days when people had hoped and prayed that his wife would still bear him a child. He had served in Shpaltov for thirteen years and had been married for three more.

But if his *kehillah* had given up, he and his pious Rebbetzin had not. The couple tried everything: while pursuing the matter along spiritual avenues, they sought to obtain medical treatment as well. But all of their efforts were to no avail.

The insensitivity of the villagers did not help matters either. They had no intention to humiliate, but they were rustic, unsophisticated folk. The woodchoppers, dairymen, and poultry farmers of Shpaltov did not know how to relate to the Rabbi's problem with tact. It was not uncommon for them to ask him some *shaila* concerning children, and then abruptly withdraw the question — apologizing for having raised the subject.

OUTWARDLY THE RABBI made light of their foibles and their overblown reactions, but inside he was aching. The Rabbi and his wife, it seemed, would have made perfect parents, since they had so much to give. Such considerations, however, only frustrated them all the more, for their hopes were in vain.

To add to their tragic situation, some of the local riffraff suggested replacing the Rabbi with a new cleric — one with a family. "A rabbi without children cannot serve and guide us properly," they argued. But this was actually just an excuse for their own inadequacies, a way to relieve their discomfort over the Rabbi's burden. The townsfolk were uneasy facing the Rabbi and his predicament daily. Therefore, instead of accepting the situation, they devised a way to avoid it.

The Rabbi and the Rebbetzin were crushed. Not only was their reaction cruel, considering all that the Rabbi did for his community, but there was a grim finality about their proposal. How could they know that the Shpaltover Rabbi and his wife would never have a child?

Sensing her husband's total dejection, the Rebbetzin suggested a last resort she had never articulated before. "Go to the *Maggid*," she urged her husband, "the holy *Maggid* of Koznitz." After sixteen years of marriage, and with trouble brewing in town, the time had come for drastic measures.

HER HUSBAND heeded her with trepidation. Who hadn't heard of the *Maggid* of Koznitz? Of his striking parables, charitable deeds, and miraculous feats! The *Maggid* was possessed of a lofty spirit which made him privy to matters beyond the ken of mortal man. Indeed, this was one of the reasons the Shpaltover Rabbi had avoided making the pilgrimage to Koznitz all along. He was inwardly afraid to subject himself to the *Maggid*'s piercing clairvoyance.

True, the Shpaltover Rabbi was too righteous and God-fearing to deserve outright censure, but the *Maggid* of Koznitz did not judge by ordinary standards. He saw all. When he traveled from town to town to give *mussar*, he admonished people not only for what they neglected to do, but also for what they could have done and were capable of achieving.

The Shpaltover Rabbi feared that the *Maggid*'s searing gaze would see right through him. Worse yet, the *Maggid* might reveal that he and his wife were not destined to bear children. They would much prefer to live with hope and disappointment than with such a devastating verdict.

It was with a heavy heart, then, that the Shpaltover Rabbi arrived in Koznitz, where he found the *Maggid* deeply engrossed in the sacred tomes. Several minutes elapsed before the *Maggid* noticed his guest, and in the interim the Shpaltover Rabbi reviewed his plan: he would not merely ask the *Maggid* for a blessing; he would explain that he had traveled all this way in a final effort to merit progeny. The Shpaltover Rabbi was determined to impress upon the *Maggid* not only his desperation but also the trust he had invested in the *Maggid*'s powers to intercede before the Master of the Universe.

When the *Maggid* finally sensed someone standing in his presence, he drew the Rabbi in with his eyes.

"Yes, my friend," he said softly, motioning for the guest to be seated on a stone bench worn smooth by broken-hearted petitioners.

The Shpaltover Rabbi related his woes, wiping his eyes dry several times during his rendition. He concluded by stating, "When we were wed we dreamed about raising a large family of devoted Jews. That was sixteen years ago. And now, aside from all of the misery this situation has caused us, my position and *parnassa* are currently in jeopardy. I have come to the *Maggid* as my final hope; we have tried everything else. Won't the *Maggid* please intervene on our behalf?"

The *Maggid* closed his eyes pensively for a few moments and then uttered in a barely audible voice: "Everyone has *tzuris*. If somehow we would be able to see the troubles that plague others, we would be grateful to God for the misfortunes that we ourselves suffer. The pain of others would be unbearable for us. Our problem is that we cannot see clearly, and we refuse to understand that God does only that which, ultimately, is right for us."

THE SHPALTOVER RABBI began to fret. He didn't travel to Koznitz for consolation; it was salvation he sought.

The *Maggid* shut his eyes again and softly tapped his finger on the table. The Shpaltover Rabbi tightened up. Every fiber of his being was now concentrated in prayer, hope and yearning that the *Maggid* would accede to his request, and that he wouldn't leave Koznitz empty-handed, to return to an anxious wife and a community of mockers...

The Belzer Rebbe hauled up the bucket of water he had filled from the well and placed it on the ledge. He wiped the sweat from his brow and rested for a few moments, simultaneously allowing the suspense of the story to build up. The chassidim didn't move; they remained transfixed, waiting for their Rebbe to finish. Eventually Reb Aharon resumed his tale, realizing that no more water would be drawn until it was over...

After several minutes, which felt like an eternity, the *Maggid* opened his fiery eyes. They were moist.

"My friend," he told the Shpaltover Rabbi, "I see that all of the gates of Heaven are closed for you. But there is one way: one person has the key that can unlock one of the gates."

The Shpaltover Rabbi leaned forward, waiting to hear the name, the city, and the address.

"This man," continued the *Maggid*, "actually lives near your little town."

THE SHPALTOVER RABBI was amazed. He knew all of the residents of his village and the surrounding area. He wasn't aware of anyone with even a moderately saintly personality.

The *Maggid* saw that the Shpaltover Rabbi was trying to imagine who in his area could hold the key to one of Heaven's gates. To lessen the pain of suspense he quickly revealed the secret:

"In the woods outside your village lives one of the thirty-six holy *tzaddikim* who support the world. His name is Shvartzawolf."

"Shvartzawolf?!" the Rabbi sputtered. Surely the *Maggid* must be mistaken, he thought.

"Yes, Shvartzawolf. He is one of the righteous *lamed-vav*. He can see what others cannot see, and is seen as others are not seen."

THE RABBI'S AMAZEMENT was justified: Shvartzawolf was the most notorious, eccentric vagabond known in Galicia. He was a mysterious woodchopper, and his conduct was anything but pious. He had no choice but to live in a cabin in the forest, for the villagers would not tolerate such an odious individual residing in their midst.

He was foul and disgusting, the nemesis of every Jew in Shpaltov. Even the kindhearted Shpaltover Rabbi, who had patience and concern for every Jew in the environs, had given up on Shvartzawolf. When the Rabbi had first arrived he tried to reach out to him, as he did to every Jew. His attempts were met with incredulity, laughter and scorn, but he tried nonetheless.

The Shpaltover Rabbi's philosophy was that everyone possessed a *pintele Yid*, which only needed to be located and then warmed. Once the fire was lit the kindled soul would be happy to give of itself and serve God.

"Hah!" the villagers laughed at their Rabbi. "Just try and get Shvartzawolf to give to others. He'll break your neck just for the suggestion!"

The Shpaltover Rabbi soon found out that this time his congregants weren't all that mistaken in their assessment. As they predicted, he had to abandon his overtures to the ogreish man out of fear for his life.

RETURNING FROM HIS REVERIE, the Shpaltover Rabbi bid the *Maggid* of Koznitz a grateful farewell and headed back to his village. For the duration of his trip home he pondered how he would be able to approach Shvartzawolf. The recluse spoke to no one and spurned all social interaction.

As the Shpaltover Rabbi neared the entrance to his town a plan evolved in his mind: on Friday afternoon he would go out into the woods and feign being lost. Just a few minutes before Shabbos, he would knock on Shvartzawolf's door and announce that he had forgotten his way in the forest. How could anyone be refused a place to stay for Shabbos?

The Shpaltover Rabbi informed his wife of his scheme and then sent word to the shul that he would not be in town for Shabbos. Fearing the worst, he prepared some minimal provisions to take along, just in case Shvartzawolf didn't prove to be the *tzaddik* that the *Maggid* claimed he was...

The Belzer Rebbe paused again and checked to see if he still held his chassidim's attention. The hectic, and sometimes frantic, situation in many homes prior to Pesach was stiff competition – but not now. All the chassidim were glued to their places in order to absorb each detail of the Shpaltover Rabbi's encounter with Shvartzawolf...

THAT FRIDAY AFTERNOON the Shpaltover Rabbi entered the dark forest. It was a few minutes before sundown when he knocked on Shvartzawolf's door. His heart was thumping and his breathing labored. Only the urgency of his situation and faith in the holy *Maggid* of Koznitz enabled him to persevere.

He knocked again — very lightly, afraid of confronting Shvartzawolf's repulsive face and menacing demeanor. He thought of backing out, but the desperation of his mission caused his adrenaline to flow. "This is all for my blessed wife, and, God willing, our child," the Rabbi whispered between *kapitlach* of *Tehillim*. He knocked once more, this time a little louder.

A shriek was heard from inside the house: "Go away and never come back!" Nonetheless, the unwelcome guest, his hair standing on end, continued to knock. The Shpaltover

Rabbi planted himself firmly in place, resolving not to leave until he had acquired Shvartzawolf's blessing.

Shvartzawolf's hideous wife eventually opened the door and, between epithets, screamed that she had already ordered him to leave. "Now scram," she hissed, wielding a large brass candlestick.

The candlestick gave the intruder new hope.

"But it is just a few minutes before Shabbos, and I am lost in the woods," the Rabbi pleaded. He managed to push the door ajar a bit more, whereupon he beheld the most gruesome-looking children imaginable. Never before had he seen creatures so bereft of charm.

Shvartzawolf's wife warned that her husband would be home any minute, and if he caught an intruder in their house he would not take to it kindly.

As her audience was seemingly unimpressed, the lady of the house looked the Rabbi straight in the eye and added, between clenched teeth, "Get out of this house and into the stable. But the second the stars come out on Saturday night, you'd better disappear!"

THE RABBI retreated to the stable. Alas, he was destined to spend this Shabbos with a weak old horse. How would the Sabbath Queen greet him in this dark, odorous shed? The Shpaltover Rabbi began to cry. As if his situation weren't bad enough, he now had to suffer this irreverent indignity. "Surely the Merciful One has a purpose for all of this agony," sighed the Rabbi, looking up to the rafters laden with bats. "If Shvartzawolf is truly a *tzaddik*," he thought to himself, "it must be partly due to his ability to live with such a wife."

There could be only one consolation in his present accommodations: the possibility that Shvartzawolf would somehow unlock a gate to Heaven over the course of this, the most miserable and most critical Shabbos of the Rabbi's life.

A few minutes later the Shpaltover Rabbi heard Shvartzawolf's heavy boots trudging up the path to his home. He heard the door to the cabin squeak open, followed by ominous footsteps marching briskly toward him. The Rabbi's spirits soared. "Shvartzawolf must truly be a *tzaddik* after all," he optimistically concluded, "and he is coming to invite me into his home for Shabbos."

But nothing could have been farther from his host's mind. Shvartzawolf yanked open the stable door in one swift movement and raised an intimidating fist in the direction of the Rabbi's head. Shvartzawolf had never looked so ugly and abrasive.

"You had better be gone the second Shabbos is over," he threatened in a voice of deadly calm. Shvartzawolf slammed the door and stomped back home.

The Shpaltover Rabbi now feared for his very life, a situation which made his other problem pale.

THE RABBI had brought along a little fish, some challahs and grape juice, but his lack of appetite prevented him from eating with relish. He dutifully swallowed his provisions, all the while chewing over in his mind what to make of this Shvartzawolf. Would this man be the end of him... or the key to his immortality?

For all of Shvartzawolf's violent gestures and scurrilous talk the Rabbi believed within that the *Maggid* could not be mistaken. "Only Shvartzawolf can unlock the sealed gates" — these words echoed in his ears. He knew that the *Maggid* could see what others could not. Despite appearances, he, a rabbi, had flaws to correct, and his host, reputed to be a lout, was really a holy *tzaddik* of the highest order.

The hours dragged on and night stretched into morning. The Rabbi cried a lot, laughed a little, and slept not at all. As the day waned, he desperately tried to think of a plan; Shabbos was almost over.

The Shpaltover Rabbi sat in the stable, reviewing his past and pondering his precarious future. In another hour at the very most, the sun would begin to set over the treetops, and he would have forfeited his one opportunity to receive a blessing from Shvartzawolf. He felt so helpless.

HELPLESS. The word accurately described his sixteen years of marriage. He served his equine stablemate some straw and wondered if she was privileged to have fulfilled God's primary command and blessing: "Be fruitful and multiply."

There was just one person who could open the gate for him, the *Maggid* had said. And here he was, geographically just a few meters from his salvation, but in reality a world away. Instead of singing *zemiros* with his wife, the Rabbi was holed up in a smelly stable, accompanied only by an old nag destined for the glue factory.

For sixteen years both he and his wife had had faith, day after day, year after year, that their salvation would come. The letdowns and heartbreaks were unrelenting, yet they refused to believe that they would leave this world without offspring. They had seen so many couples blessed with passels of children; couldn't the Master of the Universe spare them just one child? Would the Rabbi's line of brilliant scholars end here in this stable?

THE SHPALTOVER RABBI'S MIND reverted to his mission. The *Maggid* had assured him that Shvartzawolf was actually one of the thirty-six *tzaddikim.* "They see what others can't, and cannot be seen as others are," he had emphasized. This last, enigmatic clause troubled him. What was the *Maggid* alluding to?

"Just one more hour to go," the despondent Rabbi considered. The dreariness of this Shabbos, clearly the worst day of his life, paled before the terrible future that he feared lay in store for him.

"But why give up?" his conscience nagged. "Because I cannot approach Shvartzawolf," he answered himself. Perhaps he should run away while he still could; his plight did not take precedence over an imminent threat. No, his inner voice protested, he didn't go through all this to run away now. There were sixty minutes left, and he had to try. He had to do something.

Sinking down upon the straw-littered floor, he began to pour out his heart to the Almighty. Sparks of *teshuva* never before kindled were ignited, and he resolved to cleanse every blemish of his tarnished soul. He went over in his mind every action he had taken in the last several years, every word that he should not have spoken, and determined that the sins of his past would not be repeated. This Shabbos became Yom Kippur a hundred times over for the Rabbi.

IN THE VERY MIDST of purifying his soul he felt a soft hand touch him on his shoulder. He looked up and there stood Shvartzawolf, glittering like the High Priest when he entered the Holy of Holies. All of a sudden the *Maggid*'s ambiguous words became clear: "He cannot be seen as others are seen: because looking at him is only a reflection of oneself. The thirty-six *tzaddikim* are so spiritual that their souls mirror whoever approaches them.

Shvartzawolf was fulsome and fearsome to all those whose souls were sullied by iniquitous deeds or thoughts. But now that the Shpaltover Rabbi had elevated his *neshama* to a higher, more pious plane, he was able to see Shvartzawolf as he really was.

"Won't you please join us for *seudah shlishis*?" Shvartzawolf offered, extending his hand.

The Shpaltover Rabbi followed his host into a home that he didn't recognize. Everything was fastidiously arranged and the children, the very same obnoxious-looking kids from yesterday, now appeared cherubic. Shvartzawolf's wife was also a graceful and gracious hostess, offering him many dishes of sumptuous food.

They washed, blessed, and sat down to the most delicious feast the Shpaltover Rabbi had ever tasted. Shvartzawolf presided over his table like *Shlomo Hamelech* in his kingly court, singing psalms and *zemiros* in perfect harmony with his children.

JUST AS THE SUN was about to set, Shvartzawolf turned to his guest and said, "I know why you have come to see me. Please God, you will soon be blessed with a boy. I ask only one favor of you: that you name your son after me."

The Shpaltover Rabbi was astounded by this unusual request. His first impulse was to ask how he could name a baby after someone who was living, but he contained himself. Who was he to challenge this holy *tzaddik*?

And, in actuality, he was unable to utter a word, much less formulate a question. From the moment Shvartzawolf had declared the good tidings the Shpaltover Rabbi had been overcome with emotion. A lump had firmly lodged itself in his throat, and his eyes were wet with gratitude.

Shvartzawolf, his face radiant with the holiness of the Sabbath, turned to his guest: "Do I have your assurance?" he asked softly.

The Shpaltover Rabbi nodded his head affirmatively.

Content with the Rabbi's acquiescence, Shvartzawolf announced that it was time to *bentch* and recite the evening prayers so that their guest could quickly return home and cheer his wife with the good news.

"How can I thank you?" the Rabbi was finally able to utter, his voice cracking with emotion.

"Your assurance is your thanks," Shvartzawolf responded. "But the most important thing is to remain at the spiritual plateau to which you have ascended this evening. There is nothing more complete than a broken heart. A genuine feeling of contrition and a resolve to repent are God's most desirable sacrifices."

They *bentched* and chanted the evening prayers, and Shvartzawolf recited *Havdallah*. It was apparent to the Shpaltover Rabbi how pained Shvartzawolf was to bid the Sabbath Queen farewell. He realized that all of the thirty-six *tzaddikim* must thrive on the Sabbath, and that their sublime *neshamos* were probably starved during the week.

Nevertheless a feeling of total, absolute bliss filled the Rabbi as he departed. The joyous tidings, the security of his family's future, and a new commitment to a more spiritual existence elated his soul. The trees seemed to part before him, and he nearly floated home.

THE NEXT MORNING in shul, the Shpaltover Rabbi was alarmed by a commotion that had erupted. The *gabbai* approached each man for something and received a vehement refusal. The Rabbi was curious to know what it was that the *gabbai* was requesting. For some odd reason the *gabbai* accepted the refusals as if he had expected them.

"What is the matter?" the Rabbi asked.

"Oh, nothing really," the *gabbai* responded half-heartedly.

"But what is it that you want? I see that you are asking everyone for something."

"Yes, yes. There is going to be a funeral later this morning and I was instructed to try and gather a *minyan* for the service. I am merely going through the motions, for I realize that such a mission is an impossibility."

"A *minyan* for a funeral an impossibility?! Since when have Jews refused to perform this ultimate *chessed*?"

"You're right, but this time it is different. You see, well, what does it matter... I am not going to waste any more time over this."

"*Baruch Dayan Emmes*... who passed away?"

"I'm sorry to disappoint you, for you ask with such empathy and emotion. It was only that grisly beast who lives in the woods, that Shvartzawolf. I'm sure that his poor *neshama* was very relieved to exit his body. I just wonder why it took so long."

The *gabbai* noticed that the Rabbi was dazed, and he abruptly stopped his diatribe. "What's the matter, Rabbi?" he asked. "Had you still hoped to influence the old wretch to give something of himself to others?"

The Rabbi was thunderstruck. He understood at once Shvartzawolf's bizarre request, and his ultimate sacrifice so that he and his wife could have a child...

"My dear chassidim," concluded the Belzer Rebbe, as he removed a large bucket of water from the lip of the well, "let us hurry home. We have holiday preparations still to make.

"In Nissan we were redeemed from the bondage of Egypt, and in Nissan we will be redeemed once again. Let us not forget," he said as he turned to regard every tear-stained cheek at the well, "that there are plenty of Shvartzawolves walking the streets. They can be found in every community. And the way that we judge others is the way that we, too, will be judged. Let us prepare now for bedika, *a thorough housecleaning, in every room, shelf, and corner of our hearts."*

Heard from: Rabbi Shlomo Carlebach

Island Holiday

As THE *KITTEL*-CLAD *shaliach tzibbur* finished the final blessing before the recitation of the *Shema*, Ari Kaufman began awkwardly gathering his *tzitzis* together. He was still not fully accustomed to wearing a *tallis*, and its heavy silver *atara* — a three-month-old wedding present from his parents — made him feel especially self-conscious.

As he began reciting the *Ahavah Rabbah* prayer — "With a great love You have loved us, Hashem" — Ari's physical uneasiness reflected the spiritual distress he had been experiencing since he and his wife had traveled from their new home in Lakewood, New Jersey, to spend the first Rosh Hashanah and Yom Kippur of their married life with his parents on Long Island.

From the time the decision had been made he had come to regret it. Ever since leaving home for *mesivta* years ago, Ari had felt uncomfortable davening in the shul his parents attended. Not that there was anything halachically wrong with the shul: it had a proper *mechitzah*, a God-fearing rabbi, and a well-educated congregation of *shomrei mitzvos*. But compared to the warmth and piety of the yeshivish davening he so loved and was accustomed to, the atmosphere in his parents' shul was sterile and cold. The long, symmetrical rows of beautifully carved and generously upholstered benches appeared forbidding. He longed for the jumble of small wooden tables and the *shtenders* of the *beis midrash* where he spent most of his waking hours.

Even more troubling to Ari was the fact that the people who davened in the shul, although by and large observant, lacked the seriousness common in a yeshiva. Their plush, imposing synagogue appeared more like a social hall. Treating the davening like elevator Muzak, they milled about the spacious, carpeted room, talking with their friends and letting their modishly dressed children run wild. By contrast, the *bochurim* and *avrechim* Ari was used to davening with knew that their cluttered *beis midrash* was in reality a *Mikdash me'at*, a lesser version of the Holy Temple itself. They conducted themselves accordingly and threw themselves, body and soul into the *avodah* of prayer.

"B*A'AVUR AVOSEINU shebotchu v'choh,*" he continued — "For the sake of our Fathers who trusted in You." These words made Ari recall the conversation he had had with his young bride, Suri, in which they had decided to accept his parents' invitation for the *Yamim Noraim*.

"I know how you feel about davening in your parents' shul," Suri had said, "but I think that our responsibility of honoring our parents is more important. Don't forget, we haven't been to your parents' since *sheva brachos*."

Ari reluctantly admitted that Suri was right. His parents had made few demands on the young couple's time, understanding their need for privacy and realizing that, as always, their son's devotion to learning left him little leisure for anything else. To refuse them now would have been unreasonable, and would have caused them needless pain.

"*Ba'avur avoseinu* — For the sake of our Fathers." So he would have to walk with his father to shul once again and strain to hear the *akeida* over the din of the *machers*, shushers, and candy men. Perhaps it would be the last time he'd have to face such a *nissayon*; perhaps this sacrificial binding wouldn't be that bad.

Furthermore, Ari thought to himself, there *were* a lot of pleasant memories associated with davening at his father's side in the shul where he had grown up. It was where he had gone to *Oneg* on Shabbos afternoons, where he had attended the daily *minyan*, where he had, with a thrill he could still recall, put on *tefillin* for the very first time as his father watched proudly.

"*Avinu, Ha'av Harachaman* — Our Father, the merciful Father, have mercy upon us." Never before had Ari felt more keenly the need for a merciful Divine judgement. This Rosh Hashanah he was praying not only *ba'ado*, for himself, but *ba'ado uv'ad beiso*, on behalf of both himself and his new wife.

HE TRIED to absorb himself in prayer, to block everything out of his mind, as he beseeched the Almighty that he and his wife be blessed with children, that his new financial responsibilities not interfere with his learning, and that all would go well in the year ahead.

"*V'sain b'libeinu l'hovin* — Instill in our hearts understanding." As Ari said these words, he thought to himself that he would never be able to understand the behavior of the people around him.

During davening the night before, Ari had been amazed to hear the men seated nearby discussing the state of the stock market, the latest political scandal in New York, and even the Mets' chances of playing in the World Series. To talk about such trivialities in shul on *any* day was unacceptable. But on the first night of Rosh Hashanah! That was like a man on trial for his life interrupting his own testimony to go joke with his friends in the back of the courtroom!

Ari did his best to refrain from resenting his parents' request that he spend *Yontiff* with them. But each time he overheard another snatch of idle conversation, every time another friend of his parents' came over to him — in the middle of davening — to wish him *mazel tov* or to ask him what he was doing for a living, he could barely conceal the shudder that ran through him. He soon became convinced that, in his concern for his parents' feelings, he had made a serious error in not remaining in Lakewood for the *Yamim Noraim*.

Trying to tell himself that he was overreacting, Ari again attempted to dispel all of these thoughts from his head as he concluded the blessing "*Habocher b'amo Yisrael b'ahavah* — He who chooses His people Yisrael with love." He closed his eyes and readied himself to concentrate on the *Shema*. Just at that moment, however, he heard a loud "Shhh!" directly behind him.

Ari flinched, his concentration gone. "Why do these people insist on bringing their small children to shul?" he wondered to himself. "If they didn't bring them here, they wouldn't have to keep shushing them and annoying everyone else."

Again, Ari tried to collect his thoughts in preparation for The acceptance of God's Oneness and Kingship. But his *kavannah* was shot dead by another noisy "Shhh!"

Silently furious, Ari mentally castigated the man behind him for not simply taking his child out of shul. Then, even as the *shaliach tzibbur* finished intoning the last blessing before the *Shema* and the congregants began the first words of the holy prayer, Ari was bombarded with a barrage from behind: "Shhh! Shhh! SHHH!!"

Nearly beside himself, Ari couldn't stand it any longer. All of his misgivings about having acceded to his parents' wishes, all the ambivalence he felt toward his fellow *mispallelim*, welled up inside him and in a bursting bubble of indignation, he glared at the man behind him.

THE MAN was seated alone. His right hand covered his eyes, but there was no mistaking the look of intense effort and utter devotion on his face as he struggled to overcome a serious speech defect in order to pronounce the first word of the statement which, for generations of Jewish history, had constituted the highest expression of *Kiddush Hashem*.

Ari turned back, his reddened face buried in his new *tallis*. He joined the rest of the shul, Jews undoubtedly as meritorious as he, in proclaiming: "*Shema Yisrael, Hashem Elokeinu, Hashem Echad.*" It was to be a meaningful Rosh Hashanah for the Lakewood man on Long Island after all.

Heard from: Dr. Zvi White

Epilogue

Looking back, doesn't it make more sense to assume that an observant Jew like Yankel Helfman has an ulcer, rather than a craving for *treif*? Does it not stand to reason that the Belzer Rebbe just would not inconvenience others for selfish concerns; or that a man like Shlomo Katz would abandon the funeral of his closest friend to purchase a plant? And even if Pincus' actions always seemed to incriminate himself, he too deserves not to be condemned, with certainty, as a thief. Is there really much of a question when an observant Jew like Dr. Miller enters a taxi on Shabbos?

And, above all, Hashem who created us, sustains us and guides us with lovingkindness, even in the most harrowing situations — could He ever, ever do anything but for our good?

May He purify our hearts to see the beauty in every Jew and speedily bring forth the day when we will no longer have to wait in suspense for that grand happy ending!

Y.B.

Glossary

Glossary

The following glossary provides a partial explanation of some of the foreign words and phrases used in this book. The spelling, tense, and explanations reflect the way the specific word is used in *Courtrooms of the Mind.* Often, there are alternate spellings and meanings for the words. Foreign words and phrases which are immediately followed by a translation in the text are not included in this section.

AIN TORAH K'TORAS ERETZ YISRAEL — No learning is comparable to the learning of Torah in the Land of Israel.

AKEIDA — lit. binding; refers to the binding of Isaac

AMUD — lit. pillar; place where the CHAZZAN leads the congregation in prayer

ARON KODESH — lit. holy ark; ark containing the Torah scrolls

ASHRECHA — lit. happy are you; blessed

ATARA — silver adornment attatched to a TALLIS

AVEIRAH — sin

AVODAH — ritual worship performed in the Holy Temple

AVRAHAM AVINU — Abraham our father

AVRECH(IM) — young married Yeshiva student

BAAL AGALLA — wagon driver

BAALEI BATTIM — lay individuals

BAAL MADREIGA — individual of lofty spiritual heights

BABA METZIA — (Aram.) lit. the middle gate; tractate in Seder Nezikin of the Talmud

BARUCH HASHEM — lit. the Lord is blessed; thank God

BEDIKA — checking for CHOMETZ the night before Passover eve

BEHAIMES — (colloq. form of *behaimos)* animals

BAINONI — individual who generally refrains from sinning

BEIS HAMIKDASH — the Holy Temple

BEIS MIDRASH — house of study used for both Torah study and prayer

BEIS DIN — court of Jewish law

BENTCH — (Yid.) to bless, usually referring to the grace after meals

BENTCHING GOIMEL — (Yid., colloq.) an event over which reciting *Bircas Hagomel* is indicated; *Bircas Hagomel* is the blessing recited after being spared from harm

BIKKUR CHOLIM — visiting the sick

BIMA — platform located in the center of the synagogue, from where the Torah is read

BOCHUR(IM) — unmarried yeshiva student

BRACHA — blessing

BRIS MILAH — Jewish rite of circumcision

CHALILAH — God forbid

CHALLA — special loaves eaten on SHABBOS

CHAS V'SHALOM — God forbid

CHAZZAN — cantor; the leader of public worship

CHEDER — lit. room; yeshiva elementary school

CHESSED — deeds of lovingkindness

CHEVRA KADISHA — lit. Holy Society; a group which provides for the religious needs of the community, particularly in the area of the care and rites of the dead

CHOL HAMOED — The Intermediate days of SUKKOS and PESACH

CHOMETZ — leaven which results when either wheat, barley, spelt, rye, or oats remain in contact with water for a period of time before baking; the Torah forbids eating or deriving any benefits from *chometz* on Passover

CHUPAH — 1. wedding canopy; 2. the wedding service

CHUTZPAH — nerve, audacity

DAN L'KAF ZECHUS — judge favorably, positively; give the benefit of the doubt

DAVEN — (Yid.) pray

DINEI TORAH — (pl.) cases brought for adjudication according to Jewish law

DIVREI TORAH — Torah thoughts

DRASHA — learned discourse

EMUNAH — faith

ERETZ YISRAEL — the land of Israel

EREV — eve

EREV SHABBOS — Sabbath eve

ESROG(IM) — citron; one of the "four species" used on SUKKOS

FRUM — (Yid.) religious

GABBAI — warden of the synagogue who collects and dispenses charity

GAON(IM) — lit. brilliant one; honorific for a distinguished sage

GEMACH — contraction of *gemilus chassadim*; interest-free loan society

GEMARA — 1. commentary on the MISHNA (together they comprise the Talmud); 2. a volume of the Talmud

GLATT — (Yid.) lit. smooth; of the highest standard

GUT SHABBOS — (Yid.) a good Sabbath

HACHNASAS ORCHIM — hospitality

HAKARAS HATOV — gratitude; recognition of the good

HALACHA — Jewish law

HALEVI — it should only be

HAMOTZI — the blessing made over bread

HASHEM — lit. the Name; respectful reference to God

HAVDALLAH — lit., separation; service to conclude the Sabbath

HESDER — combined program of yeshiva study and military service in the Israeli army

KADDISH — prayer in praise of God recited by mourners for their deceased

KABBALA — the body of Jewish mystical teachings

KALLAH — bride

KAMTZAN — a miser; a spendthrift

KAPITLACH — (Yid.) chapters

KAPOTA — elegant caftan

KASHRUS — Jewish dietary laws

KAVANNAH — devotion, intent, concentration, purpose

KAVOD — glory, honor

KEHILLAH — organized community; congregation

KIDDUSH — sanctification; prayer recited over wine to usher in the Sabbath and festivals

KITTEL — pure white cloak worn by the CHAZZAN on Rosh Hashana and Yom Kippur

KLAL YISRAEL — community of Israel; all Jewry

KLEI KODESH — lit. holy vessels; individuals who fulfill religious functions

KLEZMER — musicians

KOLLEL — post-graduate yeshiva, the student body of which is usually comprised of young married students who receive stipends

KRECHZT — (Yid.) mournful sigh

KUGELS — noodle puddings

KUPAT CHOLIM — the system of socialized medicine in Israel

KVELL(ED) — (Yid.) to beam with pride

LASHON HARA — evil talk, a derogatory or damaging statement about someone

MAARIV — the evening prayer service

MAGGID — itinerant speaker of old who would dispense MUSSAR

MASHGIACH RUCHANI — dean of students in a yeshiva who acts as spiritual guide and advisor

MATZAH(OS) — unleavened bread

MAZEL TOV — congratulations

MECHALLELEI SHABBOS BEFARHESIA — brazen violators of the Sabbath

MECHITZAH — partition separting the men from the women

MENAHEL — Yeshiva dean

MEZUZAH — a small piece of parchment inscribed with a Biblical passage and affixed to the door frame

MIDDOS — character traits

MIKVE — a ritual bath used for the purpose of ritual purification

MINCHA — the afternoon prayer service

MINYAN — quorum of ten adult Jewish males; the basic unit of community for certain religious purposes, including prayer

MISHNA(IC) — the earliest codification of Jewish oral law by Rabbi Yehudah HaNasi

MITZVA(OS) (Pl.) — lit. commandments; applied to good deeds

MIZBEACH — altar

MOHEL — one who performs the religious ceremony of circumcision

MOTEK — (colloq.) sweetie

MUSSAF — the additional prayer said on Sabbath and festivals

MUSSAR — 1. school of thought emphasizing ethical performance; 2. moral teachings; 3. ethical lecture

NEBBACH — (Yid.) unfortunately

NESHAMA — soul

NISSAYON — trial of faith

OBERLEUTNANT — (Ger.) first lieutenant

OLAM HABAH — the world to come

OLAM HAZEH — this world

ONEG — lit. delight; gathering held in honor of the Sabbath

PARNASSA — livelihood

PAROCHES — curtain of the ark containing the Torah scrolls

PAYOS — sidelocks

PESACH — Passover

PIKUACH NEFESH — matter of life and death

PINTELE YID — (Yid.) the spark of a Jewish soul in every Jew, no matter how far away he is from Judaism

PIRKE AVOS — Chapters of the Fathers

PISKEI HALACHA (PSAK sing.) — halachic rulings

PORETZ — sinister non-Jewish landowner

PUSHKA — charity box

RABBANIM — rabbis

RASHI — leading commentator on the Bible and Talmud

RAV — Rabbi

REBBE(IM) — rabbi; usually a Talmud teacher; 2. instructor; 3. chassidic leader

REBBETZIN — wife of a rabbi

RECHOV — street

REFUAH SHELEIMAH — a complete recovery

ROSH HASHANAH — beginning of Jewish year

ROSH YESHIVA — YESHIVA dean

SABRA — native-born Israeli

SANDEK — individual who holds the baby during the circumcision

SANHEDRIN — the highest judicial and ecclesiastical court of the Jewish nation

SAVLANUT — patience

SEFER (SEFARIM) — book of religious content

SEUDAH SHLISHIS — the third Sabbath meal, usually begun just before sunset and lasting past nightfall

SHABBOS — the Sabbath

SHACHARIS — the morning prayer service

SHAILOS — (pl.) lit. questions; halachic queries

SHALIACH TZIBBUR — leader of the congregation in prayer

SHALOM ALEICHEM — lit. peace be upon you; greetings!

SHALOM ZACHOR — the celebration held on the Friday night following the birth of a baby boy

SHAMMAS — synagogue caretaker; rabbi's assistant

SHAS — lit. the six orders of the MISHNA; the Talmud

SHIKTZA — (Yid.) a non-Jewish female

SHEITEL — (Yid.) wig

SHEMA — prayer recited daily proclaiming the Oneness of God and affirming faith in Him and His Torah

SHEMONEH ESREI — lit. eighteen; the central prayer in Jewish liturgy which is recited three times daily

SHIDDUCH — a (matrimonial) match

SHIEGETZ — (Yid.) non-Jewish boy

SHIUR(IM) — Torah lecture

SHIVA — lit. seven; the seven day period of mourning following death

SHLEP(PING) — (Yid.) dragging, hauling

SHMATTE — (Yid.) rag

SHMUEZ — (Yid.) ethical discourse

SHNORRER — (Yid.) beggar

SHOMREI MITZVOS — (pl.) lit. observers of the commandments; religious Jews

SHTENDER — (Yid.) lectern, used in place of desks in many YESHIVOS

SHTETL — (Yid.) village

SHTIEBLACH — (Yid.) small, informal, intimate rooms for prayer and study

SHTIKEL — (Yid.) piece

SHUL — (Yid.) synagogue

SIDDUR — prayerbook

SIMCHA — lit. joy; celebration

SUKKAH — temporary dwelling which is a central requirement of the holiday of SUKKOS

SUKKOS — week-long Autumn festival during which time one dwells in a SUKKAH

TALLIS — four-cornered prayer shawl with fringes at each corner worn by men during morning prayers

TALMID(EI) CHACHAM(IM) — Torah scholars

TALMIDIM — students

TEFILLAH — prayer; prayer service

TEFILLIN — black leather boxes containing verses from the Bible bound to the arm and head of a man during morning prayers

TEHILLIM — Psalms; Book of Psalms

TESHUVA — lit. return; repentance

TICHEL — (Yid.) woman's scarf used to cover her hair

TISCH — (Yid.) Rebbe's table

TOSAFOS — early annotations and commentaries on the Talmud

TREIFE — (Yid.) lit. torn; non-kosher; unacceptable

TZADDIK — righteous man

TZAIDA LADERECH — provisions for a journey

TZEDDAKAH — charity

TZITZIS — the fringes worn by males on a four-cornered garment

TZURIS — (Yid.) troubles

YARMULKE — (Yid.) skullcap; head covering worn by religious Jews

YASHER KOACH — well done

YESHIVA — academy of Torah study

YISHUV — lit. settlement; refers to early settlement of Jews in ERETZ YISRAEL

YOM KIPPUR — the Day of Atonement

YOM TOV — holiday

YONTIFF — (Yid.) holiday

ZECHUS (ZECHUYOS) — merit

ZEIDENE — (Yid.) silk

ZEMIROS — songs traditionally sung at the Sabbath table

ZMAN — Yeshiva semester

ZRIZUS — alacrity

ZUGGER — (Yid.) speaker